The Simple Ninja Dual Zone Air Fryer
Cookbook UK

2000+ Days Super Delicious, Quick & Energy-saving Recipes Book for Beginners incl. Snacks, Side Dishes, Desserts, etc. | Ready in less than 30 Min

Elmira Rushisvili

Table of Contents

Chapter 4 Beef, Pork, and Lamb 22

Chapter 5 Poultry 30

Chapter 6 Fish and Seafood 38

Chapter 7 Desserts   46

Chapter 8 Snacks and Appetizers   51

Chapter 9 Vegetables and Sides   59

Chapter 10 Vegetarian Mains   67

INTRODUCTION

Welcome to the flavorful world of air frying with the Ninja Air Fryer Cookbook! We are delighted that you have chosen this cookbook as your culinary companion on the journey of creating delicious, healthier, and crispy meals with the incredible Ninja Air Fryer.

In this cookbook, we will take you on a gastronomic adventure, showcasing the endless possibilities and incredible versatility of the Ninja Air Fryer. Whether you're a seasoned home cook or just starting to explore the joys of air frying, this cookbook is designed to inspire, educate, and empower you to make the most of this remarkable kitchen appliance.

Air frying has revolutionized the way we cook by providing a healthier alternative to traditional frying methods. With the Ninja Air Fryer, you can achieve that perfect golden crispiness and delectable texture using up to 75% less oil than deep frying. Say goodbye to greasy dishes and hello to guilt-free indulgence. With its powerful combination of rapid air circulation and precise temperature control, the Ninja Air Fryer ensures that every bite is crispy on the outside and tender on the inside.

But air frying isn't limited to just frying. The Ninja Air Fryer opens up a world of culinary possibilities, allowing you to roast, bake, grill, and reheat a wide variety of ingredients. From crispy fries and juicy chicken wings to tender vegetables and even decadent desserts, this cookbook will guide you through an array of mouthwatering recipes that showcase the versatility of your Ninja Air Fryer.

In this cookbook, you'll find a diverse collection of recipes that span various cuisines, dietary preferences, and occasions. From quick and easy weeknight dinners to impressive appetizers and delightful sweet treats, each recipe has been carefully crafted, tested, and perfected to ensure fantastic results. We've included a range of options to satisfy different tastes and dietary needs, including vegetarian, vegan, gluten-free, and low-carb recipes.

To help you navigate the world of air frying and make the most of your Ninja Air Fryer, this cookbook also provides essential tips, techniques, and guidance. You'll discover cooking times and temperatures, insights on using the different functions of your air fryer, and advice on choosing the right accessories to enhance your cooking experience.

Whether you're cooking for yourself, your family, or entertaining guests, the Ninja Air Fryer Cookbook will be your trusted companion, offering inspiration and guidance every step of the way. It's time to unleash your culinary creativity, explore new flavors, and enjoy the benefits of healthier cooking without compromising on taste or convenience.

Thank you for choosing this cookbook, and let the delicious air frying adventures begin! Happy air frying!

Buttons Guide of Ninja Air Fryer

To make the most of your Ninja Air Fryer, it's essential to familiarize yourself with its buttons and functions. Understanding how each button works will enable you to navigate the appliance effortlessly and cook your favorite dishes with precision and ease. Let's explore the various buttons and settings of the Ninja Air Fryer:

Power Button: The power button is your starting point. Simply press it to turn on the Ninja Air Fryer. When the appliance is powered on, a light indicator will confirm that it's ready for use. Ensure that the air fryer is placed on a stable surface and properly plugged into a power source before pressing the power button.

Time and Temperature Controls: The time and temperature controls are crucial for achieving perfectly cooked meals with your Ninja Air Fryer. These buttons allow you to set the desired cooking time and temperature for each recipe. Adjust the cooking time using the "+" and "-" buttons. Increase the time by pressing the "+" button or decrease it by pressing the "-" button. Similarly, adjust the cooking temperature using the temperature control buttons, typically labeled with "+" and "-" symbols. Increase the temperature by pressing the "+" button or decrease it by pressing the "-" button. Experiment with different time and temperature settings to achieve the desired results for your recipes.

Preheat Button: The preheat button is a useful feature that allows you to preheat the Ninja Air Fryer before cooking. Preheating ensures that the appliance reaches the desired temperature before you begin cooking your ingredients. Press the preheat button and set the desired temperature using the temperature control buttons. Once the air fryer has preheated, it will alert you, and you can proceed with adding your ingredients for cooking.

Mode Selector Button: The mode selector button allows you to choose the cooking mode or function of the Ninja Air Fryer. This button is often labeled with icons representing different cooking modes, such as air fry, roast, bake, reheat, and dehydrate. Press the mode selector button to cycle through the available options and select the desired cooking mode for your recipe. Each cooking mode has specific temperature and time settings optimized for that particular function.

Start/Stop Button: The start/stop button initiates the cooking process or stops it if needed. After setting the desired time, temperature, and cooking mode, press the start/stop button to begin cooking. The Ninja Air Fryer will start the countdown timer, and you can monitor the progress on the display. If you need to stop the cooking process before the time is up, simply press the start/stop button again to halt the cooking cycle.

Additional Function Buttons: Depending on the model of your Ninja Air Fryer, you may have additional function buttons that offer specific features. These buttons can include options such as pre-programmed settings for popular recipes, defrosting functions, or specific cooking presets. Refer to the user manual provided with your air fryer to understand the functions of these additional buttons and how to utilize them effectively.

By familiarizing yourself with these buttons and their functions, you'll gain mastery over your Ninja Air Fryer and be able to cook a wide variety of dishes with confidence. Remember to consult the user manual for your specific model to understand any unique features or functions that may differ from the general guide provided here.

Benefits of Using It

Using the Ninja Air Fryer offers a multitude of benefits that enhance your cooking experience and transform the way you prepare meals. Let's explore some of the key advantages:

Healthier Cooking: The Ninja Air Fryer allows you to achieve crispy and delicious results using significantly less oil compared to traditional frying methods. By reducing oil usage, you can enjoy healthier versions of your favorite fried foods without compromising on taste or texture.

Reduced Fat Content: With the Ninja Air Fryer, you can enjoy your favorite crispy dishes with less fat. The hot air circulation technology ensures even cooking and a crispy exterior without the need for excessive oil immersion, resulting in meals with reduced fat content.

Versatility and Culinary Creativity: Beyond air frying, the Ninja Air Fryer offers a wide range of cooking options. You can roast, bake, grill, and even reheat leftovers with precision and convenience. This versatility allows you to explore a diverse array of dishes, experiment with flavors and techniques, and expand your culinary repertoire.

Time and Energy Efficiency: The Ninja Air Fryer is designed to cook food quickly and efficiently. Its rapid air circulation system ensures even cooking and reduces cooking times compared to traditional methods. Additionally, the air fryer heats up faster than a conventional oven, saving you time and energy in the kitchen.

Easy Cleanup: Cleaning up after cooking can be a tedious task, but the Ninja Air Fryer simplifies the process. The non-stick surfaces and removable parts of the air fryer make cleaning a breeze. Most components are dishwasher-safe, allowing for hassle-free maintenance and quick cleanup.

Consistent Results: The precise temperature control of the Ninja Air Fryer ensures consistent cooking results every time. Whether you're air frying, baking, or grilling, you can expect even cooking and uniform browning, resulting in delicious and visually appealing dishes.

Space-Saving Design: The compact size of the Ninja Air Fryer makes it an excellent addition to any kitchen, especially for those with limited countertop space. Its sleek design allows for easy storage and ensures that it doesn't occupy unnecessary room in your kitchen.

Family-Friendly Cooking: The Ninja Air Fryer is perfect for preparing meals for the whole family. With its large cooking capacity, you can easily prepare enough food to satisfy everyone's appetites. Plus, the quick cooking times allow for efficient meal preparation, even on busy weeknights.

By embracing the Ninja Air Fryer, you can enjoy healthier and more flavorful meals, unleash your culinary creativity, and save time and energy in the kitchen. Its versatility and user friendly features make it a must-have appliance for any cooking enthusiast. Get ready to embark on a culinary adventure and explore the endless possibilities of air frying!

Chapter 1 Breakfasts

Chapter 1 Breakfasts

Spinach and Mushroom Mini Quiche

Prep time: 10 minutes | Cook time: 15 minutes | Serves 4

1 teaspoon rapeseed oil, plus more for spraying	4 eggs, beaten
235 g roughly chopped mushrooms	120 g grated Cheddar cheese
235 g fresh baby spinach, grated	120 g grated Cheddar cheese
	¼ teaspoon salt
	¼ teaspoon black pepper

1. Spray 4 silicone baking cups with rapeseed oil and set them aside. 2. Warm 1 teaspoon of rapeseed oil in a medium sauté pan over medium heat. Sauté the mushrooms until soft, approximately 3 to 4 minutes. 3. Add the spinach to the pan and cook until wilted, about 1 to 2 minutes. Set aside the mushroom and spinach mixture. 4. In a medium bowl, whisk together the eggs, Cheddar cheese, salt, and pepper. Gently fold the mushrooms and spinach into the egg mixture. Pour ¼ of the mixture into each silicone baking cup. Place the baking cups into one of the air fryer baskets and air fry at 180°C for 5 minutes. Stir the mixture in each ramekin slightly and air fry until the egg has set, an additional 3 to 5 minutes.

Turkey Sausage Breakfast Pizza

Prep time: 15 minutes | Cook time: 24 minutes | Serves 2

4 large eggs, divided	120 g grated low-moisture
1 tablespoon water	Mozzarella or other melting cheese
½ teaspoon garlic powder	
½ teaspoon onion granules	1 link cooked turkey sausage, chopped (about 60 g)
¼ teaspoon dried oregano	
2 tablespoons coconut flour	2 sun-dried tomatoes, finely chopped
3 tablespoons grated Parmesan cheese	
	2 sping onions, thinly sliced

1. Preheat the air fryer to 200°C. Line a cake pan with parchment paper and lightly coat it with rapeseed oil. 2. In a large bowl, whisk 2 eggs with water, garlic powder, onion granules, and dried oregano. Add coconut flour, breaking up any lumps, and stir until smooth. Mix in Parmesan cheese and let the mixture rest until thick

and dough-like. 3. Transfer the mixture to the prepared pan and spread it evenly, slightly up the sides. Air fry for about 10 minutes until the crust is set but still light in color. Top with cheeses, sausage, and sun-dried tomatoes. 4. Break the remaining 2 eggs into a small bowl and slide them onto the pizza. Return the pizza to the air fryer and cook for 10 to 14 minutes until the egg whites are set and the yolks reach the desired doneness. Garnish with scallions and let it rest for 5 minutes before serving. Enjoy the delicious Turkey Sausage Breakfast Pizza.

Simple Cinnamon Toasts & Strawberry Toast

Prep time: 15 minutes | Cook time: 8 minutes

Simple Cinnamon Toasts | Serves 4

1 tablespoon salted butter	½ teaspoon vanilla extract
2 teaspoons ground cinnamon	10 bread slices
4 tablespoons sugar	

Strawberry Toast | Makes 4 toasts

4 slices bread, ½-inch thick	235 g sliced strawberries
Butter-flavoured cooking spray	1 teaspoon sugar

Prepare for Simple Cinnamon Toasts:

1. Preheat the air fryer to 190°C.
2. In a bowl, combine the butter, cinnamon, sugar, and vanilla extract. Spread onto the slices of bread.
3. Put the bread inside zone 1.

Prepare for Strawberry Toast:

1. Spray one side of each bread slice with butter-flavoured cooking spray. Lay slices sprayed side down.
2. Divide the strawberries among the bread slices
3. Sprinkle evenly with the sugar and place in zone 2 in a single layer.

Cook:

1. In zone 1, adjust the air fryer temperature to 190°C and air fry for 4 minutes, or until golden brown.
2. In zone 2, adjust the air fryer temperature to 200°C and air fry for 8 minutes.
3. Press SYNC, then press Start.

Sausage and Egg Breakfast Burrito

Prep time: 5 minutes | Cook time: 30 minutes | Serves 6

6 eggs
Salt and pepper, to taste
Cooking oil
120 g chopped red pepper
120 g chopped green pepper
230 g chicken sausage meat

(removed from casings)
120 ml tomato salsa
6 medium (8-inch) wheat tortillas
120 g grated Cheddar cheese

1. Whisk the eggs in a medium bowl and season with salt and pepper. 2. Heat a skillet over medium-high heat and spray with cooking oil. Add the eggs and scramble for 2 to 3 minutes until fluffy. Remove from the skillet and set aside. 3. If needed, spray the skillet with more oil and add chopped red and green bell peppers. Cook for 2 to 3 minutes until softened. 4. Add the sausage meat to the skillet and break it into smaller pieces using a spatula or spoon. Cook for 3 to 4 minutes until browned. 5. Stir in the tomato salsa and scrambled eggs. Remove the skillet from heat. 6. Spoon the mixture evenly onto the tortillas. 7. Fold the sides of each tortilla in toward the middle, then roll up from the bottom to form the burritos. Secure with toothpicks or moisten the outside edge of the tortilla with water. 8. Spray the burritos with cooking oil and place them in the air fryer, ensuring they are not stacked. Cook at 200ºC for 8 minutes. 9. Flip the burritos and cook for an additional 2 minutes or until crisp. 10. Repeat steps 8 and 9 if necessary for remaining burritos. 11. Sprinkle Cheddar cheese over the burritos and allow them to cool before serving. Enjoy your Sausage and Egg Breakfast Burrito.

Bacon and Spinach Egg Muffins & Savory Sweet Potato Hash

Prep time: 22 minutes | Cook time: 18 minutes

Bacon and Spinach Egg Muffins | Serves 6

6 large eggs
60 ml double (whipping) cream
½ teaspoon sea salt
¼ teaspoon freshly ground black pepper
¼ teaspoon cayenne pepper

(optional)
180 g frozen chopped spinach, thawed and drained
4 strips cooked bacon, crumbled
60 g grated Cheddar cheese

Savory Sweet Potato Hash | Serves 6

2 medium sweet potatoes, peeled and cut into 1-inch cubes
½ green pepper, diced

½ red onion, diced
110 g baby mushrooms, diced
2 tablespoons rapeseed oil

1 garlic clove, minced
½ teaspoon salt
½ teaspoon black pepper

½ tablespoon chopped fresh rosemary

Prepare for Bacon and Spinach Egg Muffins:

1. In a large bowl (with a spout if you have one), whisk together the eggs, double cream, salt, black pepper, and cayenne pepper (if using).
2. Divide the spinach and bacon among 6 silicone muffin cups. Place the muffin cups in zone 1.
3. Divide the egg mixture among the muffin cups. Top with the cheese.

Prepare for Savory Sweet Potato Hash:

1. Preheat the air fryer to 190ºC.
2. In a large bowl, toss all ingredients together until the vegetables are well coated and seasonings distributed.
3. Pour the vegetables into zone 2, making sure they are in a single even layer. (If using a smaller air fryer, you may need to do this in two batches.)

Cook:

1. In zone 1, adjust the air fryer temperature to 150ºC and air fry for 12 to 14 minutes, until the eggs are set and cooked through.
2. In zone 2, adjust the air fryer temperature to 190ºC and air fry for 9 minutes.
3. Press SYNC, then press Start.
4. For zone 2, toss or flip the vegetables. Roast for 9 minutes more. Transfer to a serving bowl or individual plates and enjoy.

Cajun Breakfast Sausage

Prep time: 10 minutes | Cook time: 15 to 20 minutes | Serves 8

680 g 85% lean turkey mince
3 cloves garlic, finely chopped
¼ onion, grated
1 teaspoon Tabasco sauce

1 teaspoon Cajun seasoning
1 teaspoon dried thyme
½ teaspoon paprika
½ teaspoon cayenne

1. Preheat the air fryer to 190ºC. 2. In a large bowl, combine turkey, garlic, onion, Tabasco, Cajun seasoning, thyme, paprika, and cayenne. Mix thoroughly with clean hands and shape into 16 patties, about ½ inch thick. Wet your hands slightly if the sausage mixture is sticky. 3. Arrange the patties in a single layer in the air fryer, half in zone 1 and the remaining in zone 2. Cook for 15 to 20 minutes, flipping the patties halfway through the cooking time. Ensure that the internal temperature reaches 74ºC using a thermometer inserted into the thickest portion. Enjoy your flavorful Cajun Breakfast Sausage.

Mushroom-and-Tomato Stuffed Hash Browns

Prep time: 10 minutes | Cook time: 20 minutes | Serves 4

rapeseed oil cooking spray
1 tablespoon plus 2 teaspoons rapeseed oil, divided
110 g baby mushrooms, diced
1 spring onion, white parts and green parts, diced

1 garlic clove, minced
475 g grated potatoes
½ teaspoon salt
¼ teaspoon black pepper
1 plum tomato, diced
120 g grated mozzarella

1. Preheat the air fryer to 190°C and lightly grease a 6-inch cake pan with rapeseed oil cooking spray. 2. Heat 2 teaspoons of rapeseed oil in a small skillet over medium heat. Add mushrooms, spring onion, and garlic, cooking for 4 to 5 minutes until softened and slightly colored. Remove from heat. 3. In a large bowl, combine potatoes, salt, pepper, and 1 tablespoon of rapeseed oil, ensuring all potatoes are coated. 4. Pour half of the potatoes into the cake pan, then layer with the mushroom mixture, tomato, and mozzarella. Spread the remaining potatoes on top. 5. Bake in the air fryer for 12 to 15 minutes until the top turns golden brown. 6. Allow the dish to cool for 5 minutes before slicing and serving the Mushroom-and-Tomato Stuffed Hash Browns.

Western Frittata

Prep time: 10 minutes | Cook time: 19 minutes | Serves 1 to 2

½ red or green pepper, cut into ½-inch chunks
1 teaspoon rapeseed oil
3 eggs, beaten
60 g grated Cheddar cheese
60 g diced cooked ham

Salt and freshly ground black pepper, to taste
1 teaspoon butter
1 teaspoon chopped fresh parsley

1. Preheat the air fryer to 200°C. 2. Toss the peppers with rapeseed oil and air fry for 6 minutes, shaking the basket occasionally. 3. In a bowl, beat the eggs well and stir in the Cheddar cheese, ham, salt, and pepper. Add the air-fried peppers to the bowl. 4. Place a cake pan with butter into the air fryer basket, using an aluminum sling to lower and remove it for greasing. Pour the egg mixture into the pan and return it to the air fryer. 5. Air fry at 190°C for 12 minutes until the frittata puffs up and turns lightly brown. Let it cool in the air fryer for 5 minutes, then remove the pan and sprinkle with parsley. Serve the Western Frittata immediately.

White Bean–Oat Waffles & Green Eggs and Ham

Prep time: 15 minutes | Cook time: 20 minutes

White Bean–Oat Waffles | Serves 2

1 large egg white
2 tablespoons finely ground flaxseed
120 ml water
¼ teaspoon salt
1 teaspoon vanilla extract
120 g cannellini beans, drained

and rinsed
1 teaspoon coconut oil
1 teaspoon liquid sweetener
120 g old-fashioned porridge oats
Extra-virgin rapeseed oil cooking spray

Green Eggs and Ham | Serves 2

1 large Hass avocado, halved and pitted
2 thin slices ham
2 large eggs
2 tablespoons chopped spring onions, plus more for garnish

½ teaspoon fine sea salt
¼ teaspoon ground black pepper
60 g grated Cheddar cheese (omit for dairy-free)

Prepare for White Bean–Oat Waffles:

1. In a blender, combine the egg white, flaxseed, water, salt, vanilla, cannellini beans, coconut oil, and sweetener. Blend on high for 90 seconds.
2. Add the oats. Blend for 1 minute more.
3. Preheat the waffle iron. The batter will thicken to the correct consistency while the waffle iron preheats.
4. Spray the heated waffle iron with cooking spray.
5. Add 180 ml batter.

Prepare for Green Eggs and Ham:

1. Preheat the air fryer to 200°C.
2. Place a slice of ham into the cavity of each avocado half. Crack an egg on top of the ham, then sprinkle on the green onions, salt, and pepper.
3. Place the avocado halves in zone 2 cut side up.

Cook:

1. In zone 1, air fry for 6 to 8 minutes.
2. In zone 2, air fry for 10 minutes, or until the egg is cooked to your desired doneness.
3. Press SYNC, then press Start.
4. For zone 1, serve hot, with your favourite sugar free topping.
5. For zone 2, top with the cheese (if using) and air fry for 30 seconds more, or until the cheese is melted. Garnish with chopped green onions. Best served fresh. Store extras in an airtight container in the fridge for up to 4 days. Reheat in a preheated 180°C air fryer for a few minutes, until warmed through.

Gluten-Free Granola Cereal

Prep time: 7 minutes | Cook time: 30 minutes | Makes 820 ml

Oil, for spraying
350 g gluten-free porridge oats
120 g chopped walnuts
120 g chopped almonds
120 g pumpkin seeds
60 ml maple syrup or honey
1 tablespoon toasted sesame oil or vegetable oil
1 teaspoon ground cinnamon
½ teaspoon salt
120 g dried cranberries

1. Preheat the air fryer to 120°C. Line one of the air fryer baskets with parchment and lightly spray it with oil to prevent the granola from falling through the holes. 2. In a large bowl, combine oats, walnuts, almonds, pumpkin seeds, maple syrup, sesame oil, cinnamon, and salt. Mix well. 3. Spread the mixture evenly in the prepared basket. 4. Cook for 30 minutes, stirring every 10 minutes to ensure even cooking. 5. Once cooked, transfer the granola to a bowl and add the dried cranberries. Toss to combine. 6. Allow the granola to cool to room temperature before storing it in an airtight container.

Jalapeño and Bacon Breakfast Pizza & Bacon, Cheese, and Avocado Melt

Prep time: 10 minutes | Cook time: 10 minutes

Jalapeño and Bacon Breakfast Pizza | Serves 2

235 ml grated Cheddar cheese
30 g soft cheese, broken into small pieces
4 slices cooked bacon, chopped
60 g chopped pickled jalapeños
1 large egg, whisked
¼ teaspoon salt

Bacon, Cheese, and Avocado Melt | Serves 2

1 avocado
4 slices cooked bacon, chopped
2 tablespoons tomato salsa
1 tablespoon double cream
60 g grated Cheddar cheese

Prepare for Jalapeño and Bacon Breakfast Pizza:

1. Place Mozzarella in a single layer on the bottom of an ungreased round nonstick baking dish. Scatter soft cheese pieces, bacon, and jalapeños over Mozzarella, then pour egg evenly around baking dish.
2. Sprinkle with salt and place into zone 1.

Prepare for Bacon, Cheese, and Avocado Melt:

1. Preheat the air fryer to 200°C.
2. Slice the avocado in half lengthwise and remove the stone. To ensure the avocado halves do not roll in the basket, slice a thin piece of skin off the base.
3. In a small bowl, combine the bacon, tomato salsa, and cream. Divide the mixture between the avocado halves and top with the cheese.
4. Place the avocado halves in zone 2.

Cook:

1. In zone 1, adjust the air fryer temperature to 170°C and air fry for 10 minutes.
2. In zone 2, adjust the air fryer temperature to 170°C and air fry for 3 to 5 minutes.
3. Press SYNC, then press Start.
4. For zone 1, when cheese is brown and egg is set, pizza will be done. Let cool on a large plate 5 minutes before serving.

Pitta and Pepperoni Pizza & Bacon Eggs on the Go

Prep time: 15 minutes | Cook time: 15 minutes

Pitta and Pepperoni Pizza | Serves 1

1 teaspoon rapeseed oil
1 tablespoon pizza sauce
1 pitta bread
6 pepperoni slices
60 g grated Cheddar cheese
¼ teaspoon garlic powder
¼ teaspoon dried oregano

Bacon Eggs on the Go | Serves 1

2 eggs
110 g bacon, cooked
Salt and ground black pepper, to taste

Prepare for Pitta and Pepperoni Pizza:

1. Preheat the air fryer to 180°C. Grease the air fryer basket with rapeseed oil.
2. Spread the pizza sauce on top of the pitta bread. Put the pepperoni slices over the sauce, followed by the Cheddar cheese.
3. Season with garlic powder and oregano.
4. Put the pitta pizza inside zone 1 and place a trivet on top.

Prepare for Bacon Eggs on the Go:

1. Preheat the air fryer to 200°C. Put liners in a regular cupcake tin.
2. Crack an egg into each of the cups and add the bacon. Season with some pepper and salt. Put in zone 2.

Cook:

1. In zone 1, adjust the air fryer temperature to 180°C and air fry for 6 minutes.
2. In zone 2, adjust the air fryer temperature to 200°C and air fry for 15 minutes.
3. Press SYNC, then press Start.

Potatoes Lyonnaise

Prep time: 10 minutes | Cook time: 31 minutes | Serves 4

1 sweet/mild onion, sliced thick
1 teaspoon butter, melted
1 teaspoon soft brown sugar
2 large white potatoes (about 450 g in total), sliced ½-inch

1 tablespoon vegetable oil
Salt and freshly ground black pepper, to taste

1. Preheat the air fryer to 190ºC. 2. Toss sliced onions with melted butter and brown sugar in one of the air fryer baskets. Air fry for 8 minutes, shaking the basket occasionally. 3. Par-cook the potatoes in boiling salted water for 3 minutes. Drain and pat dry with a kitchen towel. 4. Add the potatoes to the onions in the air fryer basket, drizzle with vegetable oil, and season with salt and pepper. Toss to coat. 5. Increase the air fryer temperature to 200ºC and air fry for 20 minutes, tossing the vegetables occasionally for even browning. 6. Season with salt and pepper, then serve the Potatoes Lyonnaise warm.

Parmesan Sausage Egg Muffins & Three-Berry Dutch Pancake

Prep time: 15 minutes | Cook time: 20 minutes

Parmesan Sausage Egg Muffins | Serves 4

170 g Italian-seasoned sausage, sliced
6 eggs
30 ml double cream

Salt and ground black pepper, to taste
85 g Parmesan cheese, grated

Three-Berry Dutch Pancake | Serves 4

2 egg whites
1 egg
60 g wholemeal plain flour plus
1 tablespoon cornflour
120 ml semi-skimmed milk
1 teaspoon pure vanilla extract

1 tablespoon unsalted butter, melted
235 g sliced fresh strawberries
120 g fresh blueberries
120 g fresh raspberries

Prepare for Parmesan Sausage Egg Muffins:

1. Preheat the air fryer to 180ºC. Grease a muffin pan.
2. Put the sliced sausage in the muffin pan.
3. Beat the eggs with the cream in a bowl and season with salt and pepper.
4. Pour half of the mixture over the sausages in the pan.
5. Sprinkle with cheese and the remaining egg mixture. Put in zone 1.

Prepare for Three-Berry Dutch Pancake:

1. In a medium bowl, use an eggbeater or hand mixer to quickly mix the egg whites, egg, flour, milk, and vanilla until well combined.
2. Use a pastry brush to grease the bottom of a baking pan with the melted butter. Immediately pour in the batter and put the basket back in zone 2.

Cook:

1. In zone 1, adjust the air fryer temperature to 180ºC and air fry for 20 minutes.
2. In zone 2, adjust the air fryer temperature to 170ºC and air fry for 12 to 16 minutes, or until the pancake is puffed and golden brown.
3. Press SYNC, then press Start.
4. For zone 2, remove the pan from the air fryer; the pancake will fall. Top with the strawberries, blueberries, and raspberries. Serve immediately.

Breakfast Cobbler

Prep time: 20 minutes | Cook time: 30 minutes | Serves 4

Filling:
280 g sausage meat, crumbled
60 g minced onions
2 cloves garlic, minced
½ teaspoon fine sea salt
½ teaspoon ground black pepper
1 (230 g) package soft cheese (or soft cheese style spread for dairy-free), softened

180 g beef or chicken stock
Biscuits:
3 large egg whites
90 g blanched almond flour
1 teaspoon baking powder
¼ teaspoon fine sea salt
2½ tablespoons very cold unsalted butter, cut into ¼-inch pieces
Fresh thyme leaves, for garnish

1. Preheat the air fryer to 200ºC. 2. In a pie pan, combine the sausage, onions, and garlic, breaking up the sausage into small pieces and spreading it evenly. Season with salt and pepper, then bake in the air fryer for 5 minutes. 3. While the sausage cooks, purée the soft cheese and stock in a food processor or blender until smooth. 4. Remove the cooked sausage from the air fryer, crumble it more, and mix it with the soft cheese mixture. Set aside. 5. For the biscuits, whip the egg whites until stiff peaks form. In a separate bowl, whisk together the almond flour, baking powder, and salt, then cut in the butter. Gently fold the flour mixture into the egg whites. 6. Scoop the biscuit dough onto the sausage mixture, creating 4 equal-sized biscuits. Cook in the air fryer for 5 minutes, then lower the temperature to 160ºC and bake for an additional 17 to 20 minutes until the biscuits turn golden brown. Garnish with fresh thyme leaves before serving. 7. Store leftovers in the refrigerator for up to 3 days and reheat in a preheated 180ºC air fryer for 5 minutes or until warmed through.

Nutty Granola

Prep time: 5 minutes | Cook time: 1 hour | Serves 4

120 g pecans, roughly chopped	2 tablespoons melted butter
120 g walnuts or almonds, roughly chopped	60 ml granulated sweetener
60 g desiccated coconut	½ teaspoon ground cinnamon
30 g almond flour	½ teaspoon vanilla extract
60 g ground flaxseed or chia seeds	¼ teaspoon ground nutmeg
2 tablespoons sunflower seeds	¼ teaspoon salt
	2 tablespoons water

1. Preheat the air fryer to 120°C and cut a piece of parchment paper to fit inside one of the air fryer baskets. 2. In a large bowl, combine nuts, coconut, almond flour, ground flaxseed or chia seeds, sunflower seeds, butter, sweetener, cinnamon, vanilla, nutmeg, salt, and water. Mix thoroughly. 3. Spread the granola mixture on the parchment paper, flattening it to an even thickness. 4. Air fry for approximately an hour or until the granola turns golden throughout. Allow it to fully cool, then break it into bite-size pieces. Store the Nutty Granola in a covered container for up to a week.

Sausage Egg Cup

Prep time: 10 minutes | Cook time: 15 minutes | Serves 6

340 g pork sausage, removed from casings	¼ teaspoon ground black pepper
6 large eggs	½ teaspoon crushed red pepper flakes
½ teaspoon salt	

1. Grease six 4-inch ramekins with cooking oil and place a portion of sausage (about 60 g) in each ramekin. Press the sausage down to cover the bottom and about ½-inch up the sides of the ramekins. Crack one egg into each ramekin, then sprinkle them evenly with salt, black pepper, and red pepper flakes. 2. Place the ramekins into the air fryer basket. Set the temperature to 180°C and the timer to 15 minutes. The egg cups will be ready when the sausage is fully cooked to at least 64°C and the egg is firm. Serve the Sausage Egg Cups warm.

Egg and Bacon Muffins & Southwestern Ham Egg Cups

Prep time: 10 minutes | Cook time: 15 minutes

Egg and Bacon Muffins | Serves 1

2 eggs	85 g grated Cheddar cheese
Salt and ground black pepper, to taste	140 g cooked bacon
1 tablespoon green pesto	1 spring onion, chopped

Southwestern Ham Egg Cups | Serves 2

4 (30 g) slices wafer-thin ham	2 tablespoons diced red pepper
4 large eggs	2 tablespoons diced brown onion
2 tablespoons full-fat sour cream	120 g grated medium Cheddar cheese
60 g diced green pepper	

Prepare for Egg and Bacon Muffins:

1. Preheat the air fryer to 180°C. Line a cupcake tin with parchment paper.

2. Beat the eggs with pepper, salt, and pesto in a bowl. Mix in the cheese.

3. Pour the eggs into the cupcake tin and top with the bacon and spring onion.

4. Put in zone 1.

Prepare for Southwestern Ham Egg Cups:

1. Place one slice of ham on the bottom of four baking cups.

2. In a large bowl, whisk eggs with sour cream. Stir in green pepper, red pepper, and onion.

3. Pour the egg mixture into ham-lined baking cups. Top with Cheddar. Place cups into zone 2.

Cook:

1. In zone 1, adjust the air fryer temperature to 180°C and air fry for 15 minutes, or until the egg is set.

2. In zone 2, adjust the air fryer temperature to 160°C and air fry for 12 minutes, or until the tops are browned.

3. Press SYNC, then press Start.

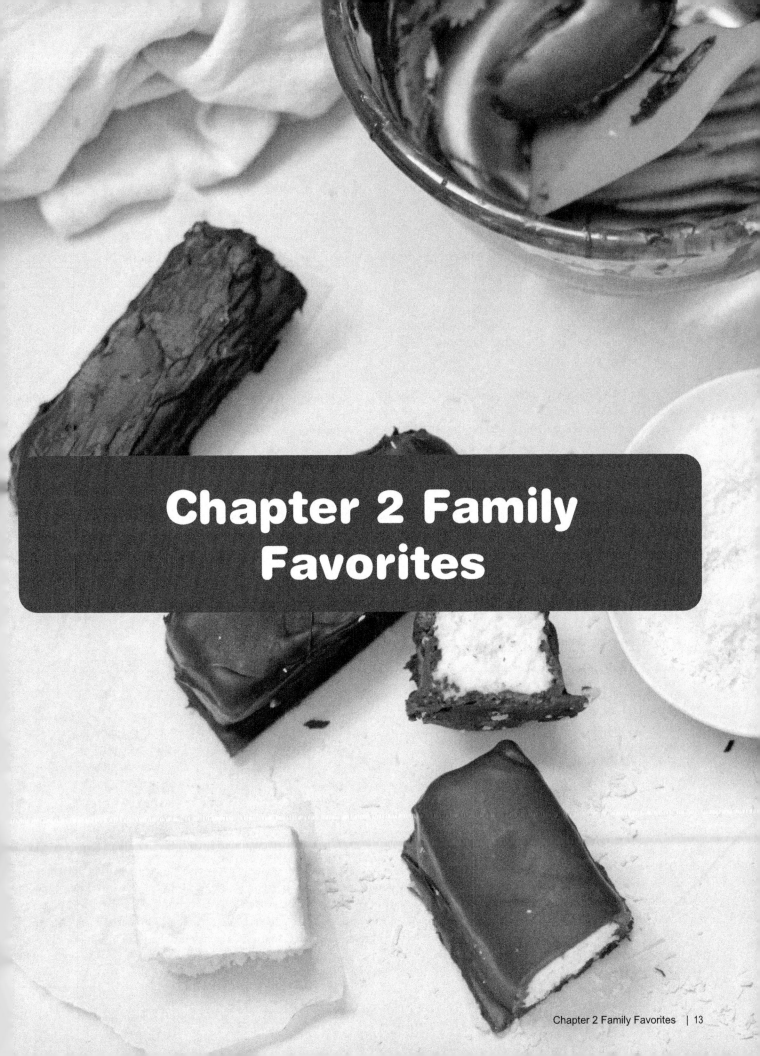

Chapter 2 Family Favorites

Chapter 2 Family Favorites

Beef Jerky

Prep time: 30 minutes | Cook time: 2 hours | Serves 8

Oil, for spraying
450 g silverside, cut into thin, short slices
60 ml soy sauce
3 tablespoons packed light
muscovado sugar
1 tablespoon minced garlic
1 teaspoon ground ginger
1 tablespoon water

1. Line the air fryer basket with parchment paper and lightly spray it with oil. 2. In a zip-top plastic bag, combine the steak, soy sauce, brown sugar, garlic, ginger, and water. Seal the bag and shake well to evenly coat the steak. 3. Refrigerate the bag for 30 minutes. Place the marinated steak in the prepared basket, ensuring a single layer half in zone 1 and the remaining in zone 2. 4. Depending on the size of your air fryer, you may need to work in batches. 5. Air fry at 80°C for at least 2 hours. 6. Adjust the cooking time to your desired level of toughness if you prefer a chewier texture. Enjoy the flavorful Beef Jerky!

Old Bay Tilapia

Prep time: 15 minutes | Cook time: 6 minutes | Serves 4

Oil, for spraying
235 ml panko breadcrumbs
2 tablespoons Old Bay or all-purpose seasoning
2 teaspoons granulated garlic
1 teaspoon onion powder
½ teaspoon salt
¼ teaspoon freshly ground black pepper
1 large egg
4 tilapia fillets

1. Preheat the air fryer to 204°C. 2. Line one of the air fryer baskets with parchment paper and lightly spray it with oil. 3. In a shallow bowl, combine breadcrumbs, seasoning, garlic, onion powder, salt, and black pepper. 4. Whisk the egg in a small bowl. 5. Dip the tilapia in the egg, then coat it in the breadcrumb mixture until fully coated. 6. Place the tilapia in the prepared basket, working in batches if necessary. 7. Lightly spray the tilapia with oil and air fry for 4 to 6 minutes, depending on the thickness of the fillets, until the internal temperature reaches 64°C. 8. Serve the Old Bay Tilapia immediately. Enjoy!

Bacon-Wrapped Hot Dogs

Prep time: 5 minutes | Cook time: 10 minutes | Serves 4

Oil, for spraying
4 bacon rashers
4 hot dog sausages
4 hot dog rolls
Toppings of choice

1. Line one of the air fryer baskets with parchment paper and lightly spray it with oil. 2. Take a strip of bacon and wrap it tightly around each hot dog, ensuring the tips are covered to prevent them from getting too crispy. 3. Secure the bacon with a toothpick at each end to prevent it from shrinking. 4. Place the bacon-wrapped hot dogs in the prepared basket. 5. Air fry at 190°C for 8 to 9 minutes, adjusting the time based on your preference for bacon crispiness. If you prefer extra-crispy bacon, cook at 200°C for 6 to 8 minutes. 6. Place the cooked hot dogs in buns, return them to the air fryer, and cook for an additional 1 to 2 minutes to warm the buns. 7. Add your desired toppings and serve the delicious Bacon-Wrapped Hot Dogs. Enjoy!

Steak Tips and Potatoes

Prep time: 10 minutes | Cook time: 20 minutes | Serves 4

Oil, for spraying
227 g baby potatoes, cut in half
½ teaspoon salt
450 g steak, cut into ½-inch pieces
1 teaspoon Worcester sauce
1 teaspoon garlic powder
½ teaspoon salt
½ teaspoon ground black pepper

1. Line one of the air fryer baskets with parchment paper and lightly spray it with oil. 2. In a microwave-safe bowl, combine the potatoes and salt, adding about ½ inch of water. 3. Microwave the potatoes for 7 minutes or until nearly tender, then drain. 4. In a large bowl, gently mix together the steak, potatoes, Worcester sauce, garlic, salt, and black pepper. 5. Spread the mixture evenly in the prepared basket and air fry at 200°C for 12 to 17 minutes, stirring after 5 to 6 minutes. 6. Adjust the cooking time based on the thickness of the meat and desired doneness. Enjoy your delicious Steak Tips and Potatoes.

Filo Vegetable Triangles

Prep time: 15 minutes | Cook time: 6 to 11 minutes | Serves 6

3 tablespoons finely chopped onion

2 garlic cloves, minced

2 tablespoons grated carrot

1 teaspoon olive oil

3 tablespoons frozen baby peas, thawed

2 tablespoons fat-free soft white cheese, at room temperature

6 sheets frozen filo pastry, thawed

Olive oil spray, for coating the dough

1. Combine onion, garlic, carrot, and olive oil in a baking pan. 2. Air fry at 200ºC for 2 to 4 minutes until the vegetables are crisp-tender. 3. Transfer the vegetables to a bowl. 4. Add peas and soft white cheese to the vegetable mixture, allowing it to cool while preparing the dough. 5. Lay one sheet of filo on a work surface and lightly spray with olive oil. 6. Layer another sheet of filo on top. Repeat with the remaining filo sheets, creating 3 stacks with 2 layers each. 7. Cut each stack lengthwise into 4 strips, resulting in 12 strips. Place a small amount of filling near the bottom of each strip. 8. Fold one corner over the filling to form a triangle, continuing to fold like a flag. 9. Seal the edge with water. Repeat with the remaining strips and filling. 10. Air fry the triangles in two batches for 4 to 7 minutes or until golden brown. Serve the delicious Filo Vegetable Triangles.

Pecan Rolls

Prep time: 20 minutes | Cook time: 20 to 24 minutes | Makes 12 rolls

220 g plain flour, plus more for dusting

2 tablespoons caster sugar, plus 60 ml, divided

1 teaspoon salt

3 tablespoons butter, at room temperature

180 ml milk, whole or semi-skimmed

40 g packed light muscovado sugar

120g chopped pecans, toasted

1 to 2 tablespoons oil

35g icing sugar (optional)

1. In a large bowl, whisk together flour, 2 tablespoons caster sugar, and salt. 2. Stir in butter and milk until a sticky dough forms. In a separate small bowl, mix brown sugar and the remaining caster sugar. 3. Place a piece of parchment paper on a floured work surface and roll the dough to ¼ inch thickness. 4. Spread the sugar mixture over the dough and sprinkle with pecans. Roll up the dough jelly roll-style, sealing the ends. 5. Cut the dough into 12 rolls. Preheat the air fryer to 160ºC. 6. Line one of the air fryer baskets with parchment paper and lightly oil the parchment. Place 6 rolls on the prepared parchment and air fry for 5 minutes. 7. Flip the rolls and air fry for an additional 5 to 7 minutes until lightly browned. Repeat with the remaining rolls. 8. Sprinkle with icing sugar, if desired. Enjoy the delicious Pecan Rolls.

Avocado and Egg Burrito & Cajun Shrimp

Prep time: 25 minutes | Cook time: 9 minutes

Avocado and Egg Burrito | Serves 4

2 hard-boiled egg whites, chopped

1 hard-boiled egg, chopped

1 avocado, peeled, pitted, and chopped

1 red pepper, chopped

3 tablespoons low-salt salsa,

plus additional for serving (optional)

1 (34 g) slice low-salt, low-fat processed cheese, torn into pieces

4 low-salt wholemeal flour wraps

Cajun Shrimp | Serves 4

Oil, for spraying

450 g king prawns, peeled and deveined

1 tablespoon Cajun seasoning

170 g Polish sausage, cut into thick slices

½ medium courgette, cut into ¼-inch-thick slices

½ medium yellow squash or butternut squash, cut into ¼-inch-thick slices

1 green pepper, seeded and cut into 1-inch pieces

2 tablespoons olive oil

½ teaspoon salt

Prepare for Avocado and Egg Burrito:

1. In a medium bowl, thoroughly mix the egg whites, egg, avocado, red pepper, salsa, and cheese.

2. Place the tortillas on a work surface and evenly divide the filling among them.

3. Fold in the edges and roll up. Secure the burritos with toothpicks if necessary.

4. Put the burritos in zone 1.

Prepare for Cajun Shrimp:

1. Preheat the air fryer to 200ºC.

2. Line zone 2 with parchment and spray lightly with oil. In a large bowl, toss together the shrimp and Cajun seasoning.

3. Add the kielbasa, courgette, squash, pepper, olive oil, and salt and mix well.

4. Transfer the mixture to the prepared basket, taking care not to overcrowd.

5. You may need to work in batches, depending on the size of your air fryer.

Cook:

1. In zone 1, adjust the air fryer temperature to 200ºC and air fry for 3 to 5 minutes, or until the burritos are light golden brown and crisp.

2. In zone 2, adjust the air fryer temperature to 2o0ºC and air fry for 9 minutes.

3. Press SYNC, then press Start.

Meatball Subs

Prep time: 15 minutes | Cook time: 19 minutes | Serves 6

Oil, for spraying
450 g 15% fat minced beef
120 ml Italian breadcrumbs (mixed breadcrumbs, Italian seasoning and salt)
1 tablespoon dried minced onion
1 tablespoon minced garlic

1 large egg
1 teaspoon salt
1 teaspoon freshly ground black pepper
6 sub rolls
1 (510 g) jar marinara sauce
350 ml shredded Mozzarella cheese

1. Preheat the air fryer to 200°C and lightly spray zone 1 with oil. 2. In a large bowl, combine minced beef, Italian breadcrumbs, dried minced onion, minced garlic, egg, salt, and black pepper. Mix well. 3. Shape the mixture into meatballs of your preferred size. 4. Place the meatballs evenly in zone 1 of the air fryer basket. 5. Toast the sub rolls in zone 2 until lightly crisp. 6. Air fry for 15 minutes, flipping the meatballs halfway through cooking. 7. While the meatballs cook, warm the marinara sauce. 8. Once cooked, place the meatballs in the marinara sauce and stir to coat evenly. 9. Fill each toasted sub roll with a few meatballs and sauce. 10. Top with shredded Mozzarella cheese. 11. Return the subs to zone 2 of the air fryer and air fry for 4 minutes, or until the cheese melts and becomes bubbly. 12. Serve the Meatball Subs hot and enjoy.

Chapter 3 Fast and Easy Everyday Favourites

Chapter 3 Fast and Easy Everyday Favourites

Cheesy Potato Patties

Prep time: 5 minutes | Cook time: 10 minutes | Serves 8

900 g white potatoes	½ teaspoon hot paprika
120 g finely chopped spring onions	475 g shredded Colby or Monterey Jack cheese
½ teaspoon freshly ground black pepper, or more to taste	60 ml rapeseed oil
1 tablespoon fine sea salt	235 g crushed crackers

1. Preheat the air fryer to 180ºC and boil the potatoes until they are soft. 2. Once boiled, dry and peel the potatoes, then thoroughly mash them until there are no lumps. 3. In a bowl, combine the mashed potatoes with spring onions, pepper, salt, paprika, and cheese. 4. Shape the mixture into balls using your hands and then flatten them into patties using your palm. 5. In a shallow dish, mix the rapeseed oil and crushed crackers together. 6. Coat each patty in the crumb mixture. 7. Bake the patties in the air fryer for about 10 minutes, working in multiple batches if necessary. 8. Serve the Cheesy Potato Patties hot and enjoy their deliciousness.

Air Fried Tortilla Chips

Prep time: 5 minutes | Cook time: 10 minutes | Serves 4

4 six-inch corn tortillas, cut in half and slice into thirds	¼ teaspoon rock salt
1 tablespoon rapeseed oil	Cooking spray

1. Preheat the air fryer to 180ºC. 2. Lightly spritz one of the air fryer baskets with cooking spray. 3. Brush the tortilla chips with rapeseed oil on a clean work surface, ensuring they are evenly coated. 4. Transfer the oiled chips to the preheated air fryer. 5. Air fry the chips for about 10 minutes, or until they become crunchy and lightly browned. 6. Halfway through the cooking time, shake the basket and sprinkle the chips with salt for added flavor. 7. Once done, transfer the crispy chips onto a plate lined with paper towels to absorb any excess oil. 8. Serve the Air Fried Tortilla Chips immediately and enjoy!

Air Fried Broccoli & Simple Pea Delight

Prep time: 10 minutes | Cook time: 15 minutes

Air Fried Broccoli | Serves 1

4 egg yolks	Salt and pepper, to taste
60 g melted butter	475 g broccoli florets
240 g coconut flour	

Simple Pea Delight | Serves 2 to 4

120 g flour	3 tablespoons pea protein
1 teaspoon baking powder	120 g chicken or turkey strips
3 eggs	Pinch of sea salt
235 ml coconut milk	235 g Mozzarella cheese
235 g soft white cheese	

Prepare for Air Fried Broccoli:

1. Preheat the air fryer to 200ºC. In a bowl, whisk the egg yolks and melted butter together.

2.Throw in the coconut flour, salt and pepper, then stir again to combine well.

3.Dip each broccoli floret into the mixture and place in zone 1.

Prepare for Simple Pea Delight:

1. Preheat the air fryer to 200ºC.

2. In a large bowl, mix all ingredients together using a large wooden spoon.

3. Spoon equal amounts of the mixture into muffin cups and put in zone 2.

Cook:

1. In zone 1, adjust the air fryer temperature to 200ºC and air fry for 6 minutes.

2. In zone 2, adjust the air fryer temperature to 200ºC and air fry for 15 minutes.

3. Press SYNC, then press Start.

4. For zone 1, take care when removing them from the air fryer and serve immediately.

Purple Potato Chips with Rosemary

Prep time: 10 minutes | Cook time: 9 to 14 minutes | Serves 6

235 ml Greek yoghurt
2 chipotle chillies, minced
2 tablespoons adobo or chipotle sauce
1 teaspoon paprika
1 tablespoon lemon juice
10 purple fingerling or

miniature potatoes
1 teaspoon olive oil
2 teaspoons minced fresh rosemary leaves
⅛ teaspoon cayenne pepper
¼ teaspoon coarse sea salt

1. Preheat the air fryer to 200°C. 2. In a medium bowl, mix together yoghurt, minced chillies, adobo sauce, paprika, and lemon juice. Refrigerate the mixture. 3. Wash the purple potatoes and pat them dry with paper towels. 4. Slice the potatoes lengthwise into thin slices using a mandoline, vegetable peeler, or a sharp knife. 5. Place the potato slices in a bowl and drizzle them with olive oil, tossing to ensure they are evenly coated. 6. Arrange the potato chips in the air fryer, half in zone 1 and the remaining in zone 2. Air fry for 9 to 14 minutes. 7. Use tongs to gently flip and rearrange the chips halfway through the cooking time. 8. Sprinkle the chips with fresh rosemary, cayenne pepper, and sea salt for added flavor. 9. Serve the crispy purple potato chips with the chipotle sauce on the side for dipping. Enjoy the delicious combination of flavors and textures in this tasty snack!

Baked Chorizo Scotch Eggs

Prep time:5 minutes | Cook time: 15 to 20 minutes | Makes 4 eggs

450 g Mexican chorizo or other seasoned sausage meat
4 soft-boiled eggs plus 1 raw egg

1 tablespoon water
120 ml plain flour
235 ml panko breadcrumbs
Cooking spray

1. Divide the chorizo into 4 equal portions and shape each portion into a disc. Take a soft-boiled egg and place it in the center of each chorizo disc. Wrap the chorizo around the egg, ensuring it is fully encased. Transfer the wrapped eggs to a plate and refrigerate for at least 30 minutes to firm up. 2. Preheat the air fryer to 182°C. 3. In a small plate, place the flour, and in another plate, place the panko breadcrumbs. In a bowl, beat the raw egg with 1 tablespoon of water. One by one, roll each encased egg in the flour, then dip it in the egg mixture, and finally coat it in the panko breadcrumbs. Place the coated eggs on a plate. 4. Spray the eggs with oil and place them in one of the air fryer baskets. Bake for 10 minutes, then turn them over and bake for an additional 5 to 10 minutes, until they are browned and crisp on all sides. 5. Once done, remove the baked chorizo Scotch eggs from the air fryer and serve them immediately. These delicious treats are perfect as a snack or appetizer. Enjoy the combination of flavorful chorizo and soft-boiled eggs encased in a crispy coating!

Simple and Easy Croutons & Beef Bratwursts

Prep time: 10 minutes | Cook time: 15 minutes

Simple and Easy Croutons | Serves 4

2 sliced bread
1 tablespoon olive oil

Hot soup, for serving

Beef Bratwursts | Serves 4

4 (85 g) beef bratwursts

Prepare for Simple and Easy Croutons:

1. Preheat the air fryer to 200°C.
2.Cut the slices of bread into medium-size chunks.
3.Brush zone 1 with the oil.
Prepare for Beef Bratwursts:
1. Preheat the air fryer to 190°C.
2. Place the beef bratwursts in zone 2.

Cook:

1. In zone 1, adjust the air fryer temperature to 200°C and air fry for 8 minutes.
2. In zone 2, adjust the air fryer temperature to 190°C and air fry for 15 minutes.
3. Press SYNC, then press Start.
4. For zone 2, turning once halfway through. Serve hot.

Air Fried Shishito Peppers

Prep time: 5 minutes | Cook time: 5 minutes | Serves 4

230 g shishito or Padron peppers (about 24)
1 tablespoon olive oil

Coarse sea salt, to taste
Lemon wedges, for serving
Cooking spray

1. Preheat the air fryer to 200°C. 2. Lightly spritz one of the air fryer baskets with cooking spray. 3. In a large bowl, coat the shishito peppers with olive oil, ensuring they are well coated. 4. Arrange the peppers in the preheated air fryer and air fry for approximately 5 minutes, or until the peppers become blistered and lightly charred. 5. Halfway through the cooking time, shake the basket and sprinkle the peppers with salt for added flavor. 6. Transfer the cooked peppers onto a plate and give them a squeeze of fresh lemon juice for a burst of tanginess before serving. Enjoy the Air Fried Shishito Peppers as a delightful and flavorful snack!

Cheesy Jalapeño Cornbread

Prep time: 10 minutes | Cook time: 20 minutes |
Serves 8

160 ml cornmeal

80 ml plain flour

¾ teaspoon baking powder

2 tablespoons margarine, melted

½ teaspoon rock salt

1 tablespoon granulated sugar

180 ml whole milk

1 large egg, beaten

1 jalapeño pepper, thinly sliced

80 ml shredded extra mature Cheddar cheese

Cooking spray

1. Preheat the air fryer to 152ºC and lightly coat the air fryer basket with cooking spray. 2. In a large bowl, combine all the ingredients and mix well until thoroughly combined. Pour the mixture into a baking pan. 3. Place the baking pan in the preheated air fryer and bake for about 20 minutes or until a toothpick inserted in the center of the bread comes out clean. 4. Once the cornbread is cooked, carefully remove the baking pan from the air fryer and allow the bread to cool for a few minutes before slicing and serving. This cheesy and spicy cornbread is a delicious side dish or snack that pairs well with soups, chili, or enjoyed on its own.

Peppery Brown Rice Fritters

Prep time: 10 minutes | Cook time: 8 to 10 minutes |
Serves 4

1 (284 g) bag frozen cooked brown rice, thawed

1 egg

3 tablespoons brown rice flour

80 g finely grated carrots

80 g minced red pepper

2 tablespoons minced fresh basil

3 tablespoons grated Parmesan cheese

2 teaspoons olive oil

1. Preheat the air fryer to 190ºC. 2. In a small bowl, combine the thawed rice, egg, and flour, mixing them together until well blended. 3. Stir in the carrots, pepper, basil, and Parmesan cheese. 4. Shape the mixture into 8 fritters and drizzle them with olive oil. 5. Carefully place the fritters into the air fryer basket. 6. Air fry for 8 to 10 minutes, or until the fritters turn golden brown and are cooked through. 7. Once done, serve the Peppery Brown Rice Fritters immediately. These fritters are packed with flavor and have a delightful crispy texture, making them a satisfying and delicious snack or side dish.

Cheesy Baked Grits

Prep time: 10 minutes | Cook time: 12 minutes |
Serves 6

180 ml hot water

2 (28 g) packages instant grits

1 large egg, beaten

1 tablespoon melted butter

2 cloves garlic, minced

½ to 1 teaspoon red pepper flakes

235 g shredded Cheddar cheese or jalapeño Jack cheese

1. Preheat the air fryer to 200ºC. 2. In a baking tray, combine the water, grits, egg, butter, garlic, and red pepper flakes, and mix well. 3. Stir in the shredded cheese until it is evenly incorporated into the mixture. 4. Place the baking tray in the air fryer basket and cook for approximately 12 minutes, or until the grits are fully cooked and a knife inserted near the center comes out clean. 5. Allow the baked grits to stand for 5 minutes before serving. These cheesy grits make a delicious side dish or breakfast option, and the air fryer provides a quick and convenient way to cook them to perfection.

Corn Fritters

Prep time: 15 minutes | Cook time: 8 minutes |
Serves 6

120 g self-raising flour

1 tablespoon sugar

1 teaspoon salt

1 large egg, lightly beaten

60 g buttermilk

180 g corn kernels

60 g minced onion

Cooking spray

1. Preheat the air fryer to 180ºC and line the air fryer baskets with parchment paper. 2. In a medium bowl, whisk together the flour, sugar, and salt until well blended. Stir in the egg and buttermilk to form a smooth batter. 3. Add the corn kernels and minced onion to the batter, mixing them in thoroughly. 4. Shape the corn fritter batter into 12 balls and place them on the parchment-lined baskets. 5. Spritz the fritters with oil to help them brown and bake for 4 minutes. 6. Flip the fritters, spritz them with oil again, and continue baking for another 4 minutes until they are firm and lightly browned. 7. Once cooked, serve the Corn Fritters immediately for a tasty and satisfying treat. These fritters have a crispy exterior and a tender, flavorful interior, making them a perfect side dish or appetizer option. Enjoy!

Beetroot Salad with Lemon Vinaigrette

Prep time: 10 minutes | Cook time: 12 to 15 minutes | Serves 4

6 medium red and golden beetroots, peeled and sliced
1 teaspoon olive oil
¼ teaspoon rock salt
120 g crumbled feta cheese
2 kg mixed greens

Cooking spray
Vinaigrette:
2 teaspoons olive oil
2 tablespoons chopped fresh chives
Juice of 1 lemon

1. Preheat the air fryer to 180ºC. 2. In a large bowl, toss the beetroots with olive oil and rock salt. 3. Spray one of the air fryer baskets with cooking spray and place the beetroots inside. Air fry them for 12 to 15 minutes until they become tender. 4. While the beetroots cook, prepare the lemon vinaigrette in a separate large bowl by whisking together olive oil, lemon juice, and chives. 5. Once the beetroots are cooked, remove them from the air fryer and toss them in the lemon vinaigrette. Allow them to cool for 5 minutes. 6. Finally, add crumbled feta cheese to the beetroots and serve the salad on a bed of mixed greens. This colorful and flavorful Beetroot Salad with Lemon Vinaigrette is a refreshing and healthy dish that can be enjoyed as a side or a light meal.

Scalloped Veggie Mix

Prep time: 10 minutes | Cook time: 15 minutes | Serves 4

1 Yukon Gold or other small white potato, thinly sliced
1 small sweet potato, peeled and thinly sliced
1 medium carrot, thinly sliced
60 g minced onion

3 garlic cloves, minced
180 ml 2 percent milk
2 tablespoons cornflour
½ teaspoon dried thyme

1. Preheat the air fryer to 190ºC. 2. In a baking tray, layer the potato, sweet potato, carrot, onion, and garlic. 3. In a small bowl, whisk together the milk, cornflour, and thyme until well blended. 4. Pour the milk mixture evenly over the layered vegetables in the pan. 5. Bake in the air fryer for approximately 15 minutes, or until the casserole is golden brown on top and the vegetables are tender. 6. Once cooked, serve the Scalloped Veggie Mix immediately. This dish offers a delicious combination of flavors and textures, and the air fryer provides a convenient and efficient way to cook it to perfection.

Chapter 4 Beef, Pork, and Lamb

Chapter 4 Beef, Pork, and Lamb

Saucy Beef Fingers

Prep time: 30 minutes | Cook time: 14 minutes | Serves 4

680 g rump steak
60 ml red wine
60 g fresh lime juice
1 teaspoon garlic powder
1 teaspoon onion granules
1 teaspoon celery salt
1 teaspoon mustard seeds

Coarse sea salt and ground black pepper, to taste
1 teaspoon red pepper flakes
2 eggs, lightly whisked
235 g Parmesan cheese
1 teaspoon paprika

1. In a large ceramic bowl, marinate the steak with red wine, lime juice, garlic powder, onion granules, celery salt, mustard seeds, salt, black pepper, and red pepper for 3 hours. 2. Tenderize the steak by pounding it with a mallet and cut it into 1-inch strips. 3. Whisk the eggs in a shallow bowl and mix Parmesan cheese and paprika in another bowl. 4. Dip the beef pieces into the whisked eggs, ensuring they are coated on all sides, then dredge them in the Parmesan mixture. 5. Cook the beef fingers in the air fryer at 200ºC for 14 minutes, flipping them halfway through the cooking time. 6. While the beef fingers cook, heat the reserved marinade in a saucepan over medium heat, allowing it to simmer until thoroughly warmed. Serve the cooked steak fingers with the sauce on the side. Enjoy these flavorful and tender Saucy Beef Fingers as a delicious appetizer or main dish.

Spaghetti Zoodles and Meatballs

Prep time: 30 minutes | Cook time: 11 to 13 minutes | Serves 6

450 g beef mince
1½ teaspoons sea salt, plus more for seasoning
1 large egg, beaten
1 teaspoon gelatin
180 g Parmesan cheese
2 teaspoons minced garlic
1 teaspoon Italian seasoning

Freshly ground black pepper, to taste
Avocado oil spray
Keto-friendly marinara sauce, for serving
170 g courgette noodles, made using a spiralizer or store-bought

1. Season the beef mince with salt in a large bowl. 2. In a separate bowl, sprinkle gelatin over the egg and let it sit for 5 minutes. Stir the gelatin mixture and pour it over the ground beef. Add Parmesan, garlic, and Italian seasoning. Season with salt and pepper. 4. Shape the mixture into 1½-inch meatballs and refrigerate for at least 1 hour or overnight. 5. Preheat the air fryer to 200ºC. Spray the meatballs with oil and air fry them for 4 minutes, flipping halfway through. Continue to cook for another 4 minutes until the internal temperature reaches 72ºC. 6. While the meatballs rest, heat marinara sauce in a saucepan on the stove. 7. Place courgette noodles in the air fryer and cook for 3 to 5 minutes at 200ºC. 8. To serve, place courgette noodles in bowls, top with meatballs, and pour warm marinara sauce over them. Enjoy your Spaghetti Zoodles and Meatballs!

Pork and Tricolor Vegetables Kebabs

Prep time: 1 hour 20 minutes | Cook time: 8 minutes per batch | Serves 4

For the Pork:
450 g pork steak, cut in cubes
1 tablespoon white wine vinegar
3 tablespoons steak sauce or brown sauce
60 ml soy sauce
1 teaspoon powdered chili
1 teaspoon red chili flakes
2 teaspoons smoked paprika
1 teaspoon garlic salt
For the Vegetable:

1 courgette, cut in cubes
1 butternut squash, deseeded and cut in cubes
1 red pepper, cut in cubes
1 green pepper, cut in cubes
Salt and ground black pepper, to taste
Cooking spray
Special Equipment:
4 bamboo skewers, soaked in water for at least 30 minutes

1. Combine the pork marinade ingredients in a large bowl and press the pork into the marinade. Refrigerate for at least an hour. 2. Preheat the air fryer to 190ºC and spray with cooking spray. 3. Remove the pork from the marinade and thread the pork and vegetables onto skewers, alternating between them. Season with salt and pepper. 4. Arrange the skewers in the air fryer and spray with cooking spray. Air fry for 8 minutes, flipping halfway through, until the pork is browned and the vegetables are charred and tender. Work in batches if needed. 5. Serve the Pork and Tricolor Vegetables Kebabs immediately. Enjoy!

Italian Sausages with Peppers and Onions

Prep time: 5 minutes | Cook time: 28 minutes | Serves 3

1 medium onion, thinly sliced	coconut oil
1 yellow or orange pepper, thinly sliced	1 teaspoon fine sea salt
1 red pepper, thinly sliced	6 Italian-seasoned sausages
60 ml avocado oil or melted	Dijon mustard, for serving (optional)

1. Preheat the air fryer to 200ºC. 2. In a large bowl, toss the onion and peppers with oil and salt until coated. 3. Transfer the onion and peppers to a pie pan and cook in the air fryer for 8 minutes, stirring halfway through. Set aside. 4. Spray one of the air fryer baskets with avocado oil and place the sausages in the basket. Air fry for 20 minutes, or until crispy and golden brown. In the last minute or two of cooking, add the onion and peppers to the basket to warm them through. 5. Arrange the onion and peppers on a serving platter and place the sausages on top. Serve with Dijon mustard on the side, if desired. 6. Store any leftovers in an airtight container in the fridge for up to 7 days or in the freezer for up to a month. To reheat, cook in a preheated 200ºC air fryer for 3 minutes, or until heated through. Enjoy your delicious Italian Sausages with Peppers and Onions made in the air fryer.

Buttery Pork Chops & Italian Lamb Chops with Avocado Mayo

Prep time: 10 minutes | Cook time: 12 minutes

Buttery Pork Chops | Serves 4

4 (110 g) boneless pork chops	pepper
½ teaspoon salt	2 tablespoons salted butter, softened
¼ teaspoon ground black	

Italian Lamb Chops with Avocado Mayo | Serves 2

2 lamp chops	120 ml mayonnaise
2 teaspoons Italian herbs	1 tablespoon lemon juice
2 avocados	

Prepare for Buttery Pork Chops:

1. Sprinkle pork chops on all sides with salt and pepper.
2. Place chops into ungreased zone 1 in a single layer.

Prepare for Italian Lamb Chops with Avocado Mayo:

1. Season the lamb chops with the Italian herbs, then set aside for 5 minutes.
2. Preheat zone 2 to 200ºC and place the rack inside. 3. Put the chops on the rack.

Cook:

1. In zone 1, adjust the air fryer temperature to 200ºC and air fry for 12 minutes. Pork chops will be golden and have an internal temperature of at least 64ºC when done.
2. In zone 2, adjust the air fryer temperature to 200ºC and air fry for 12 minutes.
3. Press SYNC, then press Start.
4. For zone 1, use tongs to remove cooked pork chops from air fryer and place onto a large plate. Top each chop with ½ tablespoon butter and let sit 2 minutes to melt. Serve warm.
5. For zone 2, in the meantime, halve the avocados and open to remove the pits. Spoon the flesh into a blender. Add the mayonnaise and lemon juice and pulse until a smooth consistency is achieved. Take care when removing the chops from the air fryer, then plate up and serve with the avocado mayo.

Sausage and Cauliflower Arancini

Prep time: 30 minutes | Cook time: 28 to 32 minutes | Serves 6

Avocado oil spray	85 g cream cheese
170 g Italian-seasoned sausage, casings removed	110 g Cheddar cheese, shredded
60 g diced onion	1 large egg
1 teaspoon minced garlic	60 g finely ground blanched almond flour
1 teaspoon dried thyme	60 g finely grated Parmesan cheese
Sea salt and freshly ground black pepper, to taste	Keto-friendly marinara sauce, for serving
120 g cauliflower rice	

1. Heat a large skillet over medium-high heat and spray it with oil. Cook the sausage for 7 minutes, breaking it up with a spoon. 2. Reduce the heat to medium and add the onion, cooking for 5 minutes. Then add the garlic, thyme, and salt and pepper, cooking for an additional minute. 3. Stir in the cauliflower rice and cream cheese, cooking for 7 minutes until the cheese melts and the cauliflower is tender. 4. Remove from heat and mix in the Cheddar cheese. Shape the mixture into 1½-inch balls using a cookie scoop. Place the balls on a parchment-lined baking sheet and freeze for 30 minutes. 5. Beat the egg in a shallow bowl. In another bowl, combine almond flour and Parmesan cheese. 6. Dip the cauliflower balls into the beaten egg, then coat them with the almond flour mixture. 7. Preheat the air fryer to 200ºC. Spray the cauliflower rice balls with oil and arrange them in a single layer in the air fryer basket. Air fry for 5 minutes, flip, and spray with more oil. Air fry for an additional 3 to 7 minutes until golden brown. 8. Serve the arancini warm with marinara sauce. Enjoy your delicious Sausage and Cauliflower Arancini made in the air fryer.

Greek-Style Meatloaf

Prep time: 5 minutes | Cook time: 25 minutes | Serves 6

450 g lean beef mince	1 teaspoon salt
2 eggs	1 teaspoon black pepper
2 plum tomatoes, diced	60 g mozzarella cheese,
½ brown onion, diced	shredded
60 g whole wheat bread crumbs	1 tablespoon olive oil
1 teaspoon garlic powder	Fresh chopped parsley, for
1 teaspoon dried oregano	garnish
1 teaspoon dried thyme	

1. Preheat the oven to 190ºC. 2. In a large bowl, combine the beef, eggs, tomatoes, onion, bread crumbs, garlic powder, oregano, thyme, salt, pepper, and cheese. Mix well until all the ingredients are evenly incorporated. 3. Shape the mixture into a loaf shape, flattening it to a thickness of about 1 inch. 4. Brush the top of the meatloaf with olive oil. Place half of the meatloaf in zone 1 of the air fryer and the remaining half in zone 2. Cook for 25 minutes. 5. Once cooked, remove the meatloaf from the air fryer and let it rest for 5 minutes. Sprinkle some parsley on top. Slice and serve. Enjoy your flavorful Greek-Style Meatloaf!

Kielbasa Sausage with Pineapple and Peppers & Chuck Kebab with Rocket

Prep time: 45 minutes | Cook time: 25 minutes

Kielbasa Sausage with Pineapple and Peppers | Serves 2 to 4

340 g kielbasa sausage, cut into	1 tablespoon barbecue
½-inch slices	seasoning
1 (230 g) can pineapple chunks	1 tablespoon soy sauce
in juice, drained	Cooking spray
235 g pepper chunks	

Chuck Kebab with Rocket | Serves 4

120 g leeks, chopped	½ teaspoon ground sumac
2 garlic cloves, smashed	3 saffron threads
900 g beef mince	2 tablespoons loosely packed
Salt, to taste	fresh flat-leaf parsley leaves
¼ teaspoon ground black	4 tablespoons tahini sauce
pepper, or more to taste	110 g baby rocket
1 teaspoon cayenne pepper	1 tomato, cut into slices

Prepare for Kielbasa Sausage with Pineapple and Peppers:

1. Preheat the air fryer to 200ºC. Spritz zone 1 with cooking spray.
2. Combine all the ingredients in a large bowl. Toss to mix well.

3. Pour the sausage mixture in the preheated air fryer.

Prepare for Chuck Kebab with Rocket:

1. In a bowl, mix the chopped leeks, garlic, beef mince, and spices; knead with your hands until everything is well incorporated.
2. Now, mound the beef mixture around a wooden skewer into a pointed-ended sausage. Put in zone 2.

Cook:

1. In zone 1, adjust the air fryer temperature to 200ºC and air fry for 10 minutes, or until the sausage is lightly browned and the pepper and pineapple are soft. Shake the basket halfway through.
2. In zone 2, adjust the air fryer temperature to 180ºC and air fry for 25 minutes.
3. Press SYNC, then press Start.

Apple Cornbread Stuffed Pork Loin

Prep time: 15 minutes | Cook time: 1 hour | Serves 4 to 6

4 strips of bacon, chopped	2 tablespoons butter
1 Granny Smith apple, peeled,	1 shallot, minced
cored and finely chopped	1 Granny Smith apple, peeled,
2 teaspoons fresh thyme leaves	cored and finely chopped
60 g chopped fresh parsley	3 sprigs fresh thyme
475 g cubed cornbread	2 tablespoons flour
120 g chicken stock	235 g chicken stock
Salt and freshly ground black	120 ml apple cider
pepper, to taste	Salt and freshly ground black
1 (900 g) boneless pork loin	pepper, to taste
Apple Gravy:	

1. Preheat the air fryer to 200ºC. 2. Cook the bacon in the air fryer until crispy. In a bowl, combine the apple, fresh thyme, parsley, cornbread, and chicken stock. Season with salt and pepper. Add the cooked bacon to the mixture. 3. Butterfly the pork loin by slicing into it lengthwise, stopping before cutting all the way through. Open up the pork loin like a book and season the inside with salt and pepper. 4. Spread the cornbread mixture onto the butterflied pork loin, leaving a border. Roll up the pork loin to enclose the stuffing, tying it with kitchen twine or securing with toothpicks. Season the outside with salt and pepper. 5. Preheat the air fryer to 180ºC. Place the stuffed pork loin in the air fryer and cook for 15 minutes. Flip and cook for another 15 minutes. Turn a quarter turn and cook for another 15 minutes. Finally, turn over to expose the fourth side and cook for 10 more minutes until the pork reaches an internal temperature of 68ºC. 7. While the pork rests, make the apple gravy by sautéing shallot, apple, and thyme in butter. Add flour, then whisk in stock and apple cider. Bring to a boil to thicken and season with salt and pepper. 8. Let the pork rest for 5 minutes before slicing. Serve with apple gravy poured over the top. Enjoy your Apple Cornbread Stuffed Pork Loin!

Super Bacon with Meat

Prep time: 5 minutes | Cook time: 1 hour | Serves 4

30 slices thick-cut bacon

110 g Cheddar cheese, shredded

340 g steak

280 g pork sausage meat

Salt and ground black pepper, to taste

1. Preheat the air fryer to 200ºC. 2. Lay out 30 slices of bacon in a woven pattern and bake until crisp. Place cheese in the center of the bacon. 3. Combine steak and sausage to form a meaty mixture. 4. Lay out the meat in a rectangle of similar size to the bacon strips and season with salt and pepper. 5. Roll the meat into a tight roll and refrigerate. 6. Preheat the air fryer to 200ºC. 7. Make a 7x7 bacon weave and roll it over the meat diagonally. 8. Bake for 60 minutes or until the internal temperature reaches at least 74ºC. 9. Let the Super Bacon with Meat rest for 5 minutes before serving. Enjoy!

Beef Steak Fingers & Chorizo and Beef Burger

Prep time: 15 minutes | Cook time: 15 minutes

Beef Steak Fingers | Serves 4

4 small beef minute steaks

Salt and ground black pepper, to taste

60 g flour

Cooking spray

Chorizo and Beef Burger | Serves 4

340 g 80/20 beef mince

110 g Mexican-style chorizo crumb

60 g chopped onion

5 slices pickled jalapeños,

chopped

2 teaspoons chili powder

1 teaspoon minced garlic

¼ teaspoon cumin

Prepare for Beef Steak Fingers:

1. Preheat the air fryer to 200ºC.
2. Cut minute steaks into 1-inch-wide strips.
3. Sprinkle lightly with salt and pepper to taste.
4. Roll in flour to coat all sides.
5. Spritz air fryer basket with cooking spray.
6. Put steak strips in zone 1 in a single layer.

Prepare for Chorizo and Beef Burger:

1. In a large bowl, mix all ingredients. Divide the mixture into four sections and form them into burger patties.
2. Place burger patties into zone 2, working in batches if necessary.

Cook:

1. In zone 1, adjust the air fryer temperature to 200ºC and air fry for 4 minutes, turn strips over, and spritz with cooking spray.

2. In zone 2, adjust the air fryer temperature to 190ºC and air fry for 15 minutes.
3. Press SYNC, then press Start.
4. For zone 1, air fry 4 more minutes and test with fork for doneness. Steak fingers should be crispy outside with no red juices inside. Serve immediately.
5. For zone 2, flip the patties halfway through the cooking time. Serve warm.

Rosemary Ribeye Steaks

Prep time: 10 minutes | Cook time: 15 minutes | Serves 2

60 g butter

1 clove garlic, minced

Salt and ground black pepper, to taste

1½ tablespoons balsamic vinegar

60 g rosemary, chopped

2 ribeye steaks

1. In a skillet, melt the butter over medium heat and fry the garlic until fragrant. 2. Remove the skillet from heat and add salt, pepper, and vinegar. Let it cool. 3. Add rosemary to the mixture and transfer everything to a Ziploc bag. 4. Place the ribeye steaks in the bag and shake well to coat the meat. Refrigerate for an hour, then let them sit for an additional twenty minutes. 5. Preheat the air fryer to 200ºC. 6. Air fry the ribeye steaks for 15 minutes. 7. Carefully remove the steaks from the air fryer and plate them. 8. Serve the Rosemary Ribeye Steaks immediately. Enjoy!

Air Fryer Chicken-Fried Steak

Prep time: 5 minutes | Cook time: 20 minutes | Serves 4

450 g beef braising steak

700 ml low-fat milk, divided

1 teaspoon dried thyme

1 teaspoon dried rosemary

2 medium egg whites

120 g gluten-free breadcrumbs

60 g coconut flour

1 tablespoon Cajun seasoning

1. Marinate the steak in 475 ml of milk for 30 to 45 minutes. 2. Remove the steak from the milk, season it with thyme and rosemary, and discard the milk. 3. In a shallow bowl, beat the egg whites with the remaining 235 ml of milk. 4. In a separate shallow bowl, combine the breadcrumbs, coconut flour, and seasoning. 5. Dip the steak in the egg white mixture, then coat it well with the breadcrumb mixture. 6. Place the coated steak in the basket of an air fryer. 7. Set the air fryer to 200ºC and cook for 10 minutes. 8. Flip the steak, close the air fryer, and cook for another 10 minutes. Let the steak rest for 5 minutes before serving. Enjoy the crispy and flavorful Air Fryer Chicken-Fried Steak!

Filipino Crispy Pork Belly

Prep time: 20 minutes | Cook time: 30 minutes | Serves 4

450 g pork belly
700 ml water
6 garlic cloves
2 tablespoons soy sauce
1 teaspoon coarse or flaky salt
1 teaspoon black pepper
2 bay leaves

1. Cut the pork belly into three thick chunks for even cooking. 2. In an Instant Pot or electric pressure cooker, combine the pork, water, garlic, soy sauce, salt, pepper, and bay leaves. Cook at high pressure for 15 minutes, then let the pressure naturally release for 10 minutes before manually releasing the remaining pressure. Alternatively, simmer the ingredients in a covered saucepan for about 1 hour until the pork is tender. 3. Carefully transfer the cooked pork to a wire rack set over a baking sheet and let it drain and dry for 10 minutes. 4. Slice each chunk of pork belly into two long slices and arrange them in the air fryer basket. Set the air fryer to 200°C and cook for 15 minutes, or until the pork fat has crisped. 5. Serve the Filipino Crispy Pork Belly immediately. Enjoy the crispy and flavorful dish!

Lebanese Malfouf (Stuffed Cabbage Rolls)

Prep time: 15 minutes | Cook time: 33 minutes | Serves 4

1 head green cabbage
450 g lean beef mince
120 g long-grain brown rice
4 garlic cloves, minced
1 teaspoon salt
½ teaspoon black pepper
1 teaspoon ground cinnamon
2 tablespoons chopped fresh mint
Juice of 1 lemon
Olive oil cooking spray
120 ml beef stock
1 tablespoon olive oil

1. Cut the cabbage in half, remove the core, and separate 12 larger leaves to use for the rolls. 2. Boil a pot of salted water and blanch the cabbage leaves for 3 minutes. Remove them from the water and set aside. 3. In a large bowl, combine beef, rice, garlic, salt, pepper, cinnamon, mint, and lemon juice, and mix well. Divide the mixture into 12 equal portions. 4. Preheat the air fryer to 180°C and lightly coat a small casserole dish with olive oil spray. 5. Place a cabbage leaf on a clean surface and spoon a portion of the beef mixture onto one side. Fold the perpendicular sides inward and roll tightly, similar to a burrito. Place the rolls in the baking dish, stacking if necessary. 6. Pour beef stock between the rolls and brush the tops with olive oil. 7. Bake the dish in the air fryer for 30 minutes. Enjoy the flavorful Lebanese Malfouf served warm.

Honey-Baked Pork Loin

Prep time: 30 minutes | Cook time: 22 to 25 minutes | Serves 6

60 ml honey
60 g freshly squeezed lemon juice
2 tablespoons soy sauce
1 teaspoon garlic powder
1 (900 g) pork loin
2 tablespoons vegetable oil

1. Whisk together honey, lemon juice, soy sauce, and garlic powder in a bowl. Set aside half of the mixture for basting. 2. Make 5 slits in the pork loin and place it in a resealable bag. Add the remaining honey mixture, seal the bag, and refrigerate for at least 2 hours to marinate. 3. Preheat the air fryer to 200°C and line the baskets with parchment paper. 4. Remove the pork from the marinade and place it on the parchment. Spritz with oil and baste with the reserved marinade. 5. Cook for 15 minutes, then flip the pork, baste again, and spritz with oil. Cook for an additional 7 to 10 minutes until the internal temperature reaches 64°C. Allow the pork to rest for 5 minutes before serving. Enjoy your flavorful Honey-Baked Pork Loin from the air fryer.

Meat and Rice Stuffed Peppers

Prep time: 20 minutes | Cook time: 18 minutes | Serves 4

340 g lean beef mince
110 g lean pork mince
60 g onion, minced
1 (425 g) can finely-chopped tomatoes
1 teaspoon Worcestershire sauce
1 teaspoon barbecue seasoning
1 teaspoon honey
½ teaspoon dried basil
120 g cooked brown rice
½ teaspoon garlic powder
½ teaspoon oregano
½ teaspoon salt
2 small peppers, cut in half, stems removed, deseeded
Cooking spray

1. Preheat the air fryer to 180°C and spray a baking tray with cooking spray. 2. Cook the beef, pork, and onion in the baking tray in the air fryer for 8 minutes, breaking up the meat halfway through. 3. In a saucepan, mix together the tomatoes, Worcestershire sauce, barbecue seasoning, honey, and basil. 4. Transfer the cooked meat mixture to a large bowl and add the cooked rice, garlic powder, oregano, salt, and 60 ml of the tomato mixture. Mix well. 5. Stuff the pepper halves with the meat and rice mixture, then arrange them in the air fryer. Air fry for 10 minutes or until the peppers are lightly charred. 6. Serve the stuffed peppers with the remaining tomato sauce on top. Enjoy your delicious Meat and Rice Stuffed Peppers cooked to perfection in the air fryer!

Fillet with Crispy Shallots

Prep time: 30 minutes | Cook time: 18 to 20 minutes | Serves 6

680 g beef fillet steaks
Sea salt and freshly ground
black pepper, to taste

4 medium shallots
1 teaspoon olive oil or avocado
oil

1. Season both sides of the steaks with salt and pepper, and let them sit at room temperature for 45 minutes. 2. Preheat the air fryer to 200ºC for 5 minutes. 3. Place the steaks in a single layer in the air fryer, with half of the steaks in zone 1 and the remaining in zone 2. Air fry for 5 minutes, then flip and cook for another 5 minutes, or until the desired level of doneness is reached (49ºC for medium-rare, for example). Remove the steaks and let them rest, tented with aluminum foil. 4. Reduce the air fryer temperature to 150ºC. Toss the shallots with oil in a medium bowl, then place them in the air fryer basket. Air fry for 5 minutes, toss them, and cook for an additional 3 to 5 minutes until crispy and golden brown. 5. Plate the steaks and arrange the crispy shallots on top. Enjoy your Fillet with Crispy Shallots!

Roast Beef with Horseradish Cream

Prep time: 5 minutes | Cook time: 35 to 45 minutes | Serves 6

900 g beef roasting joint
1 tablespoon salt
2 teaspoons garlic powder
1 teaspoon freshly ground black
pepper
1 teaspoon dried thyme
Horseradish Cream:

80 ml double cream
80 ml sour cream
80 g grated horseradish
2 teaspoons fresh lemon juice
Salt and freshly ground black
pepper, to taste

1. Preheat the air fryer to 200ºC. 2. Season the beef with salt, garlic powder, black pepper, and thyme. Place the beef in the air fryer basket, fat-side down, and lightly coat it with olive oil. Air fry for 35 to 45 minutes, turning the meat halfway through, until it reaches your desired level of doneness. Let the beef rest for 10 minutes before slicing. 3. In a small bowl, whisk together the double cream, sour cream, horseradish, and lemon juice to make the horseradish cream. Season with salt and pepper. Serve the horseradish cream alongside the sliced roast beef. Enjoy the delicious combination of flavors!

Bacon and Cheese Stuffed Pork Chops & Cheese Crusted Chops

Prep time: 20 minutes | Cook time: 12 minutes

Bacon and Cheese Stuffed Pork Chops | Serves 4

15 g plain pork scratchings,
finely crushed
120 g shredded sharp Cheddar
cheese
4 slices cooked bacon,

crumbled
4 (110 g) boneless pork chops
½ teaspoon salt
¼ teaspoon ground black
pepper

Cheese Crusted Chops | Serves 4 to 6

¼ teaspoon pepper
½ teaspoons salt
4 to 6 thick boneless pork chops
235 g pork scratching crumbs
¼ teaspoon chili powder
½ teaspoons onion granules

1 teaspoon smoked paprika
2 beaten eggs
3 tablespoons grated Parmesan
cheese
Cooking spray

Prepare for Bacon and Cheese Stuffed Pork Chops:

1. In a small bowl, mix pork scratchings, Cheddar, and bacon.
2. Make a 3-inch slit in the side of each pork chop and stuff with ¼ pork rind mixture. Sprinkle each side of pork chops with salt and pepper.
3. Place pork chops into ungreased zone 1, stuffed side up.

Prepare for Cheese Crusted Chops:

1. Preheat the air fryer to 210ºC.
2. Rub the pepper and salt on both sides of pork chops.
3. In a food processor, pulse pork scratchings into crumbs. Mix crumbs with chili powder, onion granules, and paprika in a bowl.
4. Beat eggs in another bowl.
5. Dip pork chops into eggs then into pork scratchings crumb mixture.
6. Spritz zone 2 with cooking spray and add pork chops to the basket.

Cook:

1. In zone 1, adjust the air fryer temperature to 200ºC and air fry for 12 minutes.
2. In zone 2, adjust the air fryer temperature to 210ºC and air fry for 12 minutes.
3. Press SYNC, then press Start.
4. For zone 1, pork chops will be browned and have an internal temperature of at least 64ºC when done.

Blackened Cajun Pork Roast

Prep time: 20 minutes | Cook time: 33 minutes | Serves 4

900 g bone-in pork loin roast
2 tablespoons oil
60 ml Cajun seasoning
120 g diced onion

120 g diced celery
120 g diced green pepper
1 tablespoon minced garlic

1. Make 5 slits across the pork roast and spritz it with oil, ensuring it's fully coated. Sprinkle Cajun seasoning evenly over the roast. 2. In a medium bowl, combine onion, celery, green pepper, and garlic. Set aside. 3. Preheat the air fryer to 180ºC and line one of the baskets with parchment paper. 4. Place the seasoned pork roast on the parchment and spritz with oil. 5. Cook for 5 minutes, flip the roast, and cook for another 5 minutes. Continue flipping and cooking in 5-minute intervals for a total of 20 minutes. 6. Increase the air fryer temperature to 200ºC. 7. Cook the roast for an additional 8 minutes, flip it, and add the vegetable mixture to the basket. Cook for a final 5 minutes. Allow the roast to rest for 5 minutes before serving. Enjoy the flavorful Blackened Cajun Pork Roast from the air fryer.

Chapter 5 Poultry

Chapter 5 Poultry

Tex-Mex Chicken Roll-Ups

Prep time: 10 minutes | Cook time: 14 to 17 minutes | Serves 8

900 g boneless, skinless chicken breasts or thighs
1 teaspoon chili powder
½ teaspoon smoked paprika
½ teaspoon ground cumin
Sea salt and freshly ground
black pepper, to taste
170 g Monterey Jack cheese, shredded
115 g canned diced green chilies
Avocado oil spray

1. Place the chicken between plastic wrap or in a zip-top bag and pound it until it's about ¼ inch thick. 2. In a small bowl, mix together chili powder, smoked paprika, cumin, salt, and pepper. Season both sides of the chicken with this mixture. 3. Sprinkle Monterey Jack cheese and diced green chilies onto the chicken. 4. Roll up the chicken from the long side, securing it with toothpicks and tucking in the ends. 5. Preheat the air fryer to 180ºC, spray the chicken with avocado oil, and cook it for 7 minutes. Flip the chicken and cook for an additional 7 to 10 minutes until it reaches an internal temperature of 70ºC. 6. Let the chicken rest for 5 minutes before serving. Enjoy these flavorful Tex-Mex chicken roll-ups!

Bacon-Wrapped Chicken Breasts Rolls

Prep time: 10 minutes | Cook time: 15 minutes | Serves 4

15 g chopped fresh chives
2 tablespoons lemon juice
1 teaspoon dried sage
1 teaspoon fresh rosemary leaves
15 g fresh parsley leaves
4 cloves garlic, peeled
1 teaspoon ground fennel
3 teaspoons sea salt
½ teaspoon red pepper flakes
4 (115 g) boneless, skinless chicken breasts, pounded to ¼ inch thick
8 slices bacon
Sprigs of fresh rosemary, for garnish
Cooking spray

1. Preheat the oven to 180ºC and lightly grease a muffin tin. 2. In a skillet, heat olive oil over medium heat. Add chopped mushrooms and sauté until golden brown. Add minced garlic and spinach, cooking until wilted. Remove from heat and set aside. 3. In a mixing bowl, whisk together eggs, milk, grated cheese, salt, and pepper. Stir in the cooked mushroom and spinach mixture. 4. Pour the egg mixture into the greased muffin tin, filling each cup about two-thirds full. Bake for 20-25 minutes, or until the quiches are set and golden on top. Remove from the oven and let them cool for a few minutes before removing from the tin. Serve warm and enjoy!

Sesame Chicken Breast

Prep time: 10 minutes | Cook time: 18 minutes | Serves 6

Oil, for spraying
2 (170 g) boneless, skinless chicken breasts, cut into bite-size pieces
30 g cornflour plus 1 tablespoon
60 ml soy sauce
2 tablespoons packed light
brown sugar
2 tablespoons pineapple juice
1 tablespoon molasses
½ teaspoon ground ginger
1 tablespoon water
2 teaspoons sesame seeds

1. Line the air fryer baskets with parchment paper and lightly spray with oil. 2. Place the chicken breast and cornflour in a zip-top plastic bag, seal it, and shake well to coat the chicken evenly. 3. Arrange the coated chicken in a single layer in the air fryer baskets, working in batches if needed. Spray the chicken with oil. 4. In zone 1 of the air fryer, select the Air Fry button, adjust the temperature to 200ºC, and set the time to 9 minutes. In zone 2, select the Match Cook function and press Start. Flip the chicken halfway through the cooking time, spray with more oil, and cook for another 8 to 9 minutes, or until the internal temperature reaches 76ºC. 5. While the chicken cooks, prepare the sauce by combining soy sauce, brown sugar, pineapple juice, molasses, and ginger in a small saucepan over medium heat. Stir frequently until the brown sugar dissolves. 6. In a small bowl, mix water and the remaining tablespoon of cornflour, then pour it into the soy sauce mixture. 7. Bring the sauce to a boil, stirring frequently, until it thickens. Remove from heat. 8. Transfer the cooked chicken to a large bowl, add the sauce, and toss until the chicken is evenly coated. Sprinkle with sesame seeds and serve. Enjoy your delicious Sesame Chicken Breast!

Spice-Rubbed Turkey Breast

Prep time: 5 minutes | Cook time: 45 to 55 minutes | Serves 10

1 tablespoon sea salt
1 teaspoon paprika
1 teaspoon onion powder
1 teaspoon garlic powder
½ teaspoon freshly ground

black pepper
1.8 kg bone-in, skin-on turkey breast
2 tablespoons unsalted butter, melted

1. In a small bowl, combine salt, paprika, onion powder, garlic powder, and pepper to make a spice rub. 2. Sprinkle the spice rub all over the turkey breast and brush it with some melted butter. 3. Place the turkey breast in the air fryer, with half of it in zone 1 and the remaining portion in zone 2. In zone 1, select the Air Fry button, adjust the temperature to 180°C, and set the time to 25 minutes. In zone 2, select the Match Cook function and press Start. 4. After 25 minutes, flip the turkey breast and brush it with the remaining butter. Continue cooking for an additional 20 to 30 minutes, or until an instant-read thermometer reads 70°C when inserted into the thickest part of the turkey breast. 5. Remove the turkey breast from the air fryer, tent it with aluminum foil, and let it rest for about 5 minutes before serving. Enjoy your flavorful Spice-Rubbed Turkey Breast!

Yellow Curry Chicken Thighs with Peanuts

Prep time: 10 minutes | Cook time: 20 minutes | Serves 6

120 ml unsweetened full-fat coconut milk
2 tablespoons yellow curry paste
1 tablespoon minced fresh ginger

1 tablespoon minced garlic
1 teaspoon kosher salt
450 g boneless, skinless chicken thighs, halved crosswise
2 tablespoons chopped peanuts

1. In a large bowl, combine coconut milk, curry paste, ginger, garlic, and salt to create a marinade. Add the chicken to the bowl and toss well to coat. Marinate at room temperature for 30 minutes or refrigerate for up to 24 hours. 2. Preheat the air fryer to 190°C. 3. Transfer the marinated chicken (including the marinade) to a baking pan and place it in the air fryer basket. Bake for 20 minutes, flipping the chicken halfway through the cooking time. Use a meat thermometer to ensure the chicken reaches an internal temperature of 76°C. 4. Sprinkle the cooked chicken with chopped peanuts and serve. Enjoy the flavorful Yellow Curry Chicken Thighs with Peanuts!

Chicken and Gruyère Cordon Bleu

Prep time: 15 minutes | Cook time: 15 minutes | Serves 4

4 chicken breast filets
75 g chopped ham
75 g grated Swiss cheese, or Gruyère cheese
15 g all-purpose flour
Pinch salt

Freshly ground black pepper, to taste
½ teaspoon dried marjoram
1 egg
60 g panko bread crumbs
Olive oil spray

1. Flatten the chicken breast filets gently without tearing the meat. 2. Combine ham and cheese in a small bowl, then divide the mixture among the chicken filets. Wrap the chicken around the filling and secure with toothpicks. 3. In a shallow bowl, mix flour, salt, pepper, and marjoram. 4. Beat the egg in another bowl. 5. Spread panko on a plate. 6. Coat the chicken by dipping it first in the flour mixture, then in the beaten egg, and finally in the panko, pressing the crumbs into the chicken. 7. Preheat the air fryer to 190°C using the BAKE setting for 3 minutes. 8. Spray the crisper plate with olive oil, place the coated chicken in the air fryer basket, and spray it with olive oil. 9. Set the air fryer to 190°C for 15 minutes using the BAKE setting. 10. Once cooked, ensure the chicken reaches an internal temperature of 76°C, remove the toothpicks, and serve. Enjoy your delicious chicken and Gruyère Cordon Bleu!

Stuffed Chicken Florentine

Prep time: 10 minutes | Cook time: 20 minutes | Serves 4

3 tablespoons pine nuts
40 g frozen spinach, thawed and squeezed dry
75 g ricotta cheese
2 tablespoons grated Parmesan cheese
3 cloves garlic, minced

Salt and freshly ground black pepper, to taste
4 small boneless, skinless chicken breast halves (about 680 g)
8 slices bacon

1. Toast the pine nuts in a pan using the air fryer at 200°C for 2 to 3 minutes. Transfer the pine nuts to a mixing bowl and continue preheating the air fryer. 2. In the mixing bowl, combine spinach, ricotta, Parmesan, and garlic. Season with salt and pepper and mix well. 3. Carefully slice the chicken breasts to create a pocket without cutting all the way through. Season with salt and pepper. 4. Stuff each chicken breast with the spinach mixture and fold the top over the stuffing. Wrap each chicken breast with 2 slices of bacon. 5. Air fry the chicken in batches, if needed, for 18 to 20 minutes until the bacon is crispy and the chicken reaches an internal temperature of 76°C. Enjoy your delicious Stuffed Chicken Florentine!

Wild Rice and Kale Stuffed Chicken Thighs

Prep time: 10 minutes | Cook time: 22 minutes | Serves 4

4 boneless, skinless chicken thighs
250 g cooked wild rice
35 g chopped kale
2 garlic cloves, minced
1 teaspoon salt
Juice of 1 lemon
100 g crumbled feta
Olive oil cooking spray
1 tablespoon olive oi

1. Preheat the air fryer to 192°C. 2. Place the chicken thighs between plastic wrap and use a meat mallet or rolling pin to flatten them to about ¼-inch thickness. 3. In a medium bowl, mix together the rice, kale, garlic, salt, and lemon juice. 4. Spoon a quarter of the rice mixture onto the center of each chicken thigh, then sprinkle 2 tablespoons of feta cheese over the filling. 5. Spray one of the air fryer baskets with olive oil cooking spray. 6. Fold the sides of each chicken thigh over the filling and carefully place them seam-side down in the prepared basket. Brush the tops of the stuffed thighs with olive oil. 7. Roast the chicken thighs in the air fryer for 12 minutes, then flip them over and cook for an additional 10 minutes, or until the internal temperature reaches 76°C. Enjoy your delicious Wild Rice and Kale Stuffed Chicken Thighs!

Celery Chicken

Prep time: 10 minutes | Cook time: 15 minutes | Serves 4

120 ml soy sauce
2 tablespoons hoisin sauce
4 teaspoons minced garlic
1 teaspoon freshly ground black pepper
8 boneless, skinless chicken tenderloins
120 g chopped celery
1 medium red bell pepper, diced
Olive oil spray

1. Preheat the air fryer to 190°C and lightly spray one of the air fryer baskets with olive oil. 2. In a large bowl, combine soy sauce, hoisin sauce, garlic, and black pepper to create a marinade. Add the chicken, celery, and bell pepper to the bowl and toss them in the marinade until coated. 3. Shake off the excess marinade from the chicken and place the chicken and vegetables in the air fryer basket. Lightly spray them with olive oil. If necessary, cook them in batches. Reserve the remaining marinade. 4. Air fry the chicken and vegetables for 8 minutes, then flip the chicken over and brush it with some of the reserved marinade. Continue air frying for an additional 5 to 7 minutes, or until the chicken reaches an internal temperature of at least 76°C. Serve and enjoy your flavorful Celery Chicken.

Crisp Paprika Chicken Drumsticks & Quick Chicken Fajitas

Prep time: 15 minutes | Cook time: 22 minutes

Crisp Paprika Chicken Drumsticks | Serves 2

2 teaspoons paprika
1 teaspoon packed brown sugar
1 teaspoon garlic powder
½ teaspoon dry mustard
½ teaspoon salt
Pinch pepper
4 (140 g) chicken drumsticks, trimmed
1 teaspoon vegetable oil
1 scallion, green part only, sliced thin on bias

Quick Chicken Fajitas | Serves 2

280 g boneless, skinless chicken breast, sliced into ¼-inch strips
2 tablespoons coconut oil, melted
1 tablespoon chili powder
½ teaspoon cumin
½ teaspoon paprika
½ teaspoon garlic powder
¼ medium onion, peeled and sliced
½ medium green bell pepper, seeded and sliced
½ medium red bell pepper, seeded and sliced

Prepare for Crisp Paprika Chicken Drumsticks:

1. Preheat the air fryer to 200°C.
2. Combine paprika, sugar, garlic powder, mustard, salt, and pepper in a bowl. Pat drumsticks dry with paper towels. Using metal skewer, poke 10 to 15 holes in skin of each drumstick. Rub with oil and sprinkle evenly with spice mixture. 3. Arrange drumsticks in zone 1, spaced evenly apart, alternating ends.

Prepare for Quick Chicken Fajitas:

1. Place chicken and coconut oil into a large bowl and sprinkle with chili powder, cumin, paprika, and garlic powder. Toss chicken until well coated with seasoning.
2. Place chicken into zone 2.

Cook:

1. In zone 1, adjust the air fryer temperature to 200°C and air fry for 22 to 25 minutes, flipping chicken halfway through cooking.
2. In zone 2, adjust the air fryer temperature to 180°C and air fry for 15 minutes.
3. Press SYNC, then press Start.
4. For zone 1, transfer chicken to serving platter, tent loosely with aluminum foil, and let rest for 5 minutes. Sprinkle with scallion and serve.
5. For zone 2, add onion and peppers into the basket when the cooking time has 7 minutes remaining. Toss the chicken two or three times during cooking. Vegetables should be tender and chicken fully cooked to at least 76°C internal temperature when finished. Serve warm.

Barbecue Chicken Bites

Prep time: 5 minutes | Cook time: 19 minutes | Serves 4

Oil, for spraying
2 (170 g) boneless, skinless chicken breasts, cut into bite-size pieces

30 g all-purpose flour
1 tablespoon granulated garlic
2 teaspoons seasoned salt
280 g barbecue sauce

1. Line one of the air fryer baskets with parchment paper and lightly spray it with oil. 2. Place the chicken, flour, garlic, and seasoned salt in a zip-top plastic bag, seal it, and shake well to evenly coat the chicken. 3. Arrange the chicken in a single layer in the prepared basket and spray it liberally with oil. If needed, cook in batches depending on the air fryer size. 4. Air fry at 200ºC for 8 minutes, then flip the chicken, spray it with more oil, and cook for another 8 minutes or until the internal temperature reaches 76ºC and the juices run clear. 5. Transfer the cooked chicken to a large bowl and toss it with barbecue sauce. 6. Line the air fryer basket with fresh parchment paper, return the chicken to the basket, and cook for an additional 3 minutes. Enjoy your delicious barbecue chicken bites!

Buffalo Crispy Chicken Strips

Prep time: 15 minutes | Cook time: 13 to 17 minutes per batch | Serves 4

45 g all-purpose flour
2 eggs
2 tablespoons water
60 g seasoned panko bread crumbs
2 teaspoons granulated garlic
1 teaspoon salt
1 teaspoon freshly ground black

pepper
16 chicken breast strips, or 3 large boneless, skinless chicken breasts, cut into 1-inch strips
Olive oil spray
60 ml Buffalo sauce, plus more as needed

1. Place flour in a small bowl. 2. In another bowl, whisk eggs and water together. 3. In a third bowl, stir together panko, granulated garlic, salt, and pepper. 4. Dip each chicken strip in flour, then in the egg mixture, and finally coat it in the panko mixture, pressing the crumbs onto the chicken. 5. Preheat the air fryer to 190ºC. 6. Line the basket with parchment paper and place the coated chicken strips in a single layer. Spray the top of the chicken with olive oil. 7. Air fry at 190ºC for 17 minutes, flipping the chicken halfway through and spraying with more olive oil. 8. Ensure the chicken is golden brown, crispy, and reaches an internal temperature of 76ºC. 9. Repeat the process for any remaining chicken. 10. Transfer the cooked chicken to a bowl, drizzle with Buffalo sauce, toss to coat, and serve. Enjoy your flavorful Buffalo Crispy Chicken Strips!

Brazilian Tempero Baiano Chicken Drumsticks

Prep time: 30 minutes | Cook time: 20 minutes | Serves 4

1 teaspoon cumin seeds
1 teaspoon dried oregano
1 teaspoon dried parsley
1 teaspoon ground turmeric
½ teaspoon coriander seeds
1 teaspoon kosher salt

½ teaspoon black peppercorns
½ teaspoon cayenne pepper
60 ml fresh lime juice
2 tablespoons olive oil
680 g chicken drumsticks

1. Grind the cumin, oregano, parsley, turmeric, coriander seeds, salt, peppercorns, and cayenne in a coffee grinder or spice mill until finely ground. 2. In a small bowl, combine the ground spices with lime juice and oil. Place the chicken drumsticks in a resealable plastic bag, add the marinade, seal the bag, and massage to coat the chicken well. Let it marinate at room temperature for 30 minutes or refrigerate for up to 24 hours. 3. When ready to cook, place the drumsticks skin side up in the air fryer basket. Set the air fryer to 200ºC and cook for 20 to 25 minutes, flipping the drumsticks halfway through the cooking time. Use a meat thermometer to ensure the chicken reaches an internal temperature of 76ºC. 4. Serve the flavorful drumsticks with plenty of napkins. Enjoy!

Chicken Hand Pies

Prep time: 30 minutes | Cook time: 10 minutes per batch | Makes 8 pies

180 ml chicken broth
130 g frozen mixed peas and carrots
140 g cooked chicken, chopped
1 tablespoon cornflour

1 tablespoon milk
Salt and pepper, to taste
1 (8-count) can organic flaky biscuits
Oil for misting or cooking spray

1. Bring chicken broth to a boil in a medium saucepan, then add frozen peas, carrots, and chicken. Cook for 5 minutes. 2. Dissolve cornflour in milk and stir it into the simmering mixture. Cook until thickened. 3. Remove from heat, season with salt and pepper, and let it cool slightly. 4. Separate biscuits in half to make 16 rounds. Flatten each round to make them larger and thinner. 5. Spoon chicken filling onto 8 rounds, then place the remaining rounds on top and seal the edges by pressing and crimping with a fork. 6. Spray both sides with oil or cooking spray. 7. Cook in the air fryer at 170ºC for 10 minutes or until the biscuit dough is cooked through and golden brown. Enjoy these delicious chicken hand pies!

Chicken Breasts with Asparagus, Beans, and Rocket

160 g canned cannellini beans, rinsed	½ red onion, sliced thinly
1½ tablespoons red wine vinegar	230 g asparagus, trimmed and cut into 1-inch lengths
1 garlic clove, minced	2 (230 g) boneless, skinless chicken breasts, trimmed
2 tablespoons extra-virgin olive oil, divided	¼ teaspoon paprika
	½ teaspoon ground coriander
Salt and ground black pepper, to taste	60 g baby rocket, rinsed and drained

1. Preheat the air fryer to 200ºC. 2. Warm the beans and mix them with red wine vinegar, garlic, olive oil, salt, and black pepper in a bowl. Set aside. 3. Toss the onion with salt, black pepper, and olive oil in a separate bowl. Place the onion in the air fryer and cook for 2 minutes. Add the asparagus and cook for an additional 8 minutes until tender. Transfer the onion and asparagus to the bowl with beans. 4. In a large bowl, coat the chicken breasts with the remaining ingredients, except for the baby rocket. 5. Place the chicken breasts in the air fryer and cook for 14 minutes or until the internal temperature reaches 76ºC, flipping them halfway through. 6. Remove the chicken from the air fryer and serve on a bed of aluminum foil with the asparagus, beans, onion, and rocket. Season with salt and black pepper. Toss to combine and enjoy!

Nashville Hot Chicken

1.4 kg bone-in, skin-on chicken pieces, breasts halved crosswise	120 g heavy (whipping) cream
1 tablespoon sea salt	2 large eggs, beaten
1 tablespoon freshly ground black pepper	1 tablespoon vinegar-based hot sauce
70 g finely ground blanched almond flour	Avocado oil spray
130 g grated Parmesan cheese	115 g unsalted butter
1 tablespoon baking powder	120 ml avocado oil
2 teaspoons garlic powder, divided	1 tablespoon cayenne pepper (more or less to taste)
	2 tablespoons Xylitol

1. Season the chicken with salt and pepper. 2. In a large shallow bowl, mix together almond flour, Parmesan cheese, baking powder, and 1 teaspoon of garlic powder. 3. In a separate bowl, whisk together heavy cream, eggs, and hot sauce. 4. Dip the chicken in the egg mixture, then coat it with the almond flour mixture, pressing the breading onto the chicken. Let it sit for 15 minutes. 5. Set the air fryer to 200ºC and place the chicken in a single layer in the baskets. Spray the chicken with oil and air fry for 13 minutes. 6. Flip the chicken, spray with more oil, and reduce the air fryer temperature to 180ºC. Continue air frying for 11 to 15 minutes until the chicken reaches an internal temperature of 70ºC. 7. While the chicken cooks, heat butter, avocado oil, cayenne pepper, xylitol, and 1 teaspoon of garlic powder in a saucepan until melted and combined. 8. Remove the chicken from the air fryer, dip it in the sauce using tongs, then place it on a rack to rest for 5 minutes before serving. Enjoy your delicious Nashville Hot Chicken!

Chicken Rochambeau

1 tablespoon butter	Sauce:
4 chicken tenders, cut in half crosswise	2 tablespoons butter
Salt and pepper, to taste	25 g chopped green onions
15 g flour	50 g chopped mushrooms
Oil for misting	2 tablespoons flour
4 slices ham, ¼- to ⅜-inches thick and large enough to cover an English muffin	240 ml chicken broth
	¼ teaspoon garlic powder
2 English muffins, split	1½ teaspoons Worcestershire sauce

1. Melt 1 tablespoon of butter in a baking pan by air frying at 200ºC for 2 minutes. 2. Season chicken tenders with salt and pepper, then coat them in flour. 3. Place the coated chicken in the baking pan, ensuring all pieces are coated with melted butter. 4. Air fry the chicken at 200ºC for 5 minutes, flip the pieces, lightly spray with olive oil, and continue cooking for another 5 minutes until the chicken is cooked through. 5. While the chicken cooks, prepare the sauce by melting 2 tablespoons of butter in a medium saucepan, sautéing onions and mushrooms until tender, then stirring in flour and gradually adding broth to create a smooth gravy. 6. Add garlic powder and Worcestershire sauce to the sauce, simmering until thickened. 7. Once the chicken is cooked, set the baking pan aside. 8. Air fry ham slices in the basket at 200ºC for 5 minutes until heated and slightly sizzling. Set aside on top of the chicken. 9. Air fry English muffin halves for 1 minute until toasted. 10. Assemble the Rochambeau stacks by placing a ham slice on each English muffin half, followed by 2 pieces of chicken. 11. Air fry the stacks for 1 to 2 minutes to heat through. 12. Serve each English muffin stack on a plate and generously top with the prepared sauce. Enjoy your flavorful Chicken Rochambeau!

Crispy Dill Chicken Strips

Prep time: 30 minutes | Cook time: 10 minutes | Serves 4

2 whole boneless, skinless chicken breasts (about 450 g each), halved lengthwise
230 ml Italian dressing
110 g finely crushed crisps
1 tablespoon dried dill weed
1 tablespoon garlic powder
1 large egg, beaten
1 to 2 tablespoons oil

1. In a large resealable bag, combine the chicken and Italian dressing. Refrigerate and marinate for at least 1 hour. 2. In a shallow dish, mix together the potato chips, dill, and garlic powder. Place the beaten egg in a separate shallow dish. 3. Remove the chicken from the marinade and coat each piece with egg, then coat thoroughly with the crisp mixture. 4. Preheat the air fryer to 170ºC and line one of the air fryer baskets with parchment paper. 5. Place the coated chicken on the parchment and spritz it with oil. 6. Cook for 5 minutes, then flip the chicken, spritz with more oil, and cook for an additional 5 minutes until the chicken is crispy on the outside and no longer pink on the inside. Enjoy your delicious Crispy Dill Chicken Strips!

Ginger Turmeric Chicken Thighs & Chipotle Drumsticks

Prep time: 20 minutes | Cook time: 25 minutes

Ginger Turmeric Chicken Thighs | Serves 4

4 (115 g) boneless, skin-on chicken thighs
2 tablespoons coconut oil, melted
½ teaspoon ground turmeric
½ teaspoon salt
½ teaspoon garlic powder
½ teaspoon ground ginger
¼ teaspoon ground black pepper

Chipotle Drumsticks | Serves 4

1 tablespoon tomato paste
½ teaspoon chipotle powder
¼ teaspoon apple cider vinegar
¼ teaspoon garlic powder
8 chicken drumsticks
½ teaspoon salt
⅛ teaspoon ground black pepper

Prepare for Ginger Turmeric Chicken Thighs:

1. Place chicken thighs in a large bowl and drizzle with coconut oil. Sprinkle with remaining ingredients and toss to coat both sides of thighs.
2. Place thighs skin side up into ungreased zone 1.

Prepare for Chipotle Drumsticks:

1. In a small bowl, combine tomato paste, chipotle powder, vinegar, and garlic powder.

2. Sprinkle drumsticks with salt and pepper, then place into a large bowl and pour in tomato paste mixture. Toss or stir to evenly coat all drumsticks in mixture.
3. Place drumsticks into ungreased zone 2.

Cook:

1. In zone 1, adjust the air fryer temperature to 200ºC and air fry for 25 minutes.
2. In zone 2, adjust the air fryer temperature to 200ºC and air fry for 25 minutes.
3. Press SYNC, then press Start.
4. For zone 1, after 10 minutes, turn thighs. When 5 minutes remain, flip thighs once more. Chicken will be done when skin is golden brown and the internal temperature is at least 76ºC. Serve warm.
5. For zone 2, turning drumsticks halfway through cooking. Drumsticks will be dark red with an internal temperature of at least 76ºC when done. Serve warm.

African Piri-Piri Chicken Drumsticks

Prep time: 30 minutes | Cook time: 20 minutes | Serves 2

Chicken:
1 tablespoon chopped fresh thyme leaves
1 tablespoon minced fresh ginger
1 small shallot, finely chopped
2 garlic cloves, minced
80 ml piri-piri sauce or hot sauce
3 tablespoons extra-virgin olive oil
Zest and juice of 1 lemon
1 teaspoon smoked paprika
½ teaspoon kosher salt
½ teaspoon black pepper
4 chicken drumsticks
Glaze:
2 tablespoons butter or ghee
1 teaspoon chopped fresh thyme leaves
1 garlic clove, minced
1 tablespoon piri-piri sauce
1 tablespoon fresh lemon juice

1. In a small bowl, mix together all the marinade ingredients except the chicken. Place the chicken and marinade in a resealable plastic bag, ensuring the chicken is well coated. Refrigerate for at least 2 hours or up to 24 hours, turning the bag occasionally. 2. Preheat the air fryer to 200ºC and place the marinated chicken legs in one of the air fryer baskets. Air fry for 20 minutes, flipping the chicken halfway through to ensure even cooking. 3. While the chicken is cooking, prepare the glaze. In a small saucepan, melt the butter over medium-high heat. Add the thyme and garlic, cooking until the garlic begins to brown. Stir in the piri-piri sauce and lemon juice, then simmer for a couple of minutes. 4. Transfer the cooked chicken to a serving platter and pour the prepared glaze over the top. Serve the African Piri-Piri Chicken Drumsticks immediately and enjoy their delicious flavors!

Turkey Meatloaf

Prep time: 10 minutes | Cook time: 50 minutes | Serves 4

230 g sliced mushrooms

1 small onion, coarsely chopped

2 cloves garlic

680 g 85% lean turkey mince

2 eggs, lightly beaten

1 tablespoon tomato paste

15 g almond meal

2 tablespoons almond milk

1 tablespoon dried oregano

1 teaspoon salt

½ teaspoon freshly ground black pepper

1 Roma tomato, thinly sliced

1. Preheat the air fryer to 180ºC and lightly grease a round pan with olive oil. 2. In a food processor, pulse mushrooms, onion, and garlic until finely chopped. Transfer the vegetables to a mixing bowl. 3. Add turkey, eggs, tomato paste, almond meal, milk, oregano, salt, and black pepper to the bowl with vegetables. Gently mix until well combined. Transfer the mixture to the prepared pan and shape it into a loaf. Place tomato slices on top. 4. Air fry for 50 minutes or until the meatloaf is browned and reaches an internal temperature of 76ºC. Remove from the air fryer and let it rest for 10 minutes before slicing. Enjoy your delicious Turkey Meatloaf!

Herbed Turkey Breast with Simple Dijon Sauce

Prep time: 5 minutes | Cook time: 30 minutes | Serves 4

1 teaspoon chopped fresh sage

1 teaspoon chopped fresh tarragon

1 teaspoon chopped fresh thyme leaves

1 teaspoon chopped fresh rosemary leaves

1½ teaspoons sea salt

1 teaspoon ground black pepper

1 (900 g) turkey breast

3 tablespoons Dijon mustard

3 tablespoons butter, melted

Cooking spray

1. Preheat the air fryer to 200ºC and spritz one of the air fryer baskets with cooking spray. 2. In a small bowl, combine the herbs, salt, and black pepper. Mix well and set aside. 3. In a separate bowl, combine the Dijon mustard and butter. Stir until well mixed. 4. Rub the turkey breast with the herb mixture on a clean work surface, then brush it with the Dijon mixture. 5. Place the seasoned turkey breast in the preheated air fryer basket. Air fry for approximately 30 minutes or until the internal temperature reaches at least 76ºC when measured with an instant-read thermometer. 6. Transfer the cooked turkey breast to a large plate and slice before serving. Enjoy your flavorful Herbed Turkey Breast with Simple Dijon Sauce!

Blackened Chicken

Prep time: 10 minutes | Cook time: 20 minutes | Serves 4

1 large egg, beaten

215 g Blackened seasoning

2 whole boneless, skinless chicken breasts (about 450 g each),

halved

1 to 2 tablespoons oil

1. Set up two shallow bowls—one with beaten egg and the other with Blackened seasoning. 2. Coat each chicken piece by dipping it in the beaten egg, then the Blackened seasoning, ensuring it is thoroughly coated. 3. Preheat the air fryer to 180ºC and line one of the baskets with parchment paper. 4. Place the coated chicken pieces on the parchment and spritz them with oil. 5. Cook for 10 minutes, then flip the chicken, spritz it with oil again, and cook for an additional 10 minutes until the internal temperature reaches 76ºC and the chicken is cooked through. Allow it to rest for 5 minutes before serving. Enjoy your flavorful blackened chicken!

Chapter 6 Fish and Seafood

Chapter 6 Fish and Seafood

Cod with Creamy Mustard Sauce

Prep time: 10 minutes | Cook time: 10 minutes | Serves 4

Fish:
Olive or vegetable oil, for spraying
455 g cod fillets
2 tablespoons olive oil
1 tablespoon lemon juice
1 teaspoon salt

½ teaspoon freshly ground black pepper
Mustard Sauce:
120 ml heavy cream
3 tablespoons Dijon mustard
1 tablespoon unsalted butter
1 teaspoon salt

1. Line one of the air fryer baskets with baking paper and lightly spray it with oil. 2. Rub the cod with olive oil and lemon juice, then season it with salt and black pepper. 3. Place the cod in the prepared basket, working in batches if necessary. 4. Roast the cod at 180ºC for 5 minutes, then increase the temperature to 200ºC and cook for an additional 5 minutes, or until the fish is flaky and reaches an internal temperature of 64ºC. 5. In a small saucepan, simmer the heavy cream, mustard, butter, and salt over low heat for 3 to 4 minutes until the sauce thickens. 6. Transfer the cooked cod to a serving plate and drizzle it with the creamy mustard sauce. Serve immediately and enjoy!

Simple Buttery Cod & Tuna Avocado Bites

Prep time: 15 minutes | Cook time: 8 minutes

Simple Buttery Cod | Serves 2

2 cod fillets, 110 g each
2 tablespoons salted butter, melted

1 teaspoon Old Bay seasoning
½ medium lemon, sliced

Tuna Avocado Bites | Makes 12 bites

280 g canned tuna, drained
60 ml full-fat mayonnaise
1 stalk celery, chopped
1 medium avocado, peeled, pitted, and mashed
25 g blanched finely ground almond flour, divided
2 teaspoons coconut oil

Prepare for Simple Buttery Cod:

1. Place cod fillets into a round baking dish. Brush each fillet with butter and sprinkle with Old Bay seasoning. Lay two lemon slices on each fillet.
2. Cover the dish with foil and place into zone 1.

Prepare for Tuna Avocado Bites:

1. In a large bowl, mix tuna, mayonnaise, celery, and mashed avocado. Form the mixture into balls.
2. Roll balls in almond flour and spritz with coconut oil.
3. Place balls into zone 2.

Cook:

1. In zone 1, adjust the air fryer temperature to 180ºC and air fry for 8 minutes.
2. In zone 2, adjust the air fryer temperature to 200ºC and air fry for 7 minutes.
3. Press SYNC, then press Start.
4. For zone 1, flip halfway through the cooking time. When cooked, internal temperature should be at least 64ºC. Serve warm.
5. For zone 2, gently turn tuna bites after 5 minutes. Serve warm.

Lemony Salmon

Prep time: 30 minutes | Cook time: 10 minutes | Serves 4

680 g salmon steak
½ teaspoon grated lemon zest
Freshly cracked mixed peppercorns, to taste
80 ml lemon juice
Fresh chopped chives, for

garnish
120 ml dry white wine, or apple cider vinegar
½ teaspoon fresh coriander, chopped
Fine sea salt, to taste

1. In a deep pan, combine all the marinade ingredients (except for the salmon steak and chives) and bring it to a boil over medium-high heat. Let it reduce by half and then allow it to cool down. 2. Marinate the salmon steak in the refrigerator for about 40 minutes. Discard the marinade and transfer the fish to the preheated air fryer. 3. Air fry the salmon at 200ºC for 9 to 10 minutes. 4. Once cooked, brush the hot fish steaks with the reserved marinade, garnish them with fresh chopped chives, and serve immediately. Enjoy your flavorful lemony salmon!

Smoky Prawns and Chorizo Tapas

Prep time: 15 minutes | Cook time: 10 minutes | Serves 2 to 4

110 g Spanish (cured) chorizo, halved horizontally and sliced crosswise
230 g raw medium prawns, peeled and deveined
1 tablespoon extra-virgin olive oil
1 small shallot, halved and thinly sliced
1 garlic clove, minced
1 tablespoon finely chopped fresh oregano
½ teaspoon smoked Spanish paprika
¼ teaspoon kosher or coarse sea salt
¼ teaspoon black pepper
3 tablespoons fresh orange juice
1 tablespoon minced fresh parsley

1. Place the chorizo in a baking pan and air fry at 190ºC for 5 minutes until it starts to brown and render its fat. 2. In a large bowl, combine the prawns, olive oil, shallot, garlic, oregano, paprika, salt, and pepper, and toss to coat the prawns well. 3. Transfer the prawns to the pan with the chorizo, stirring to combine. Place the pan in the air fryer basket and cook for 10 minutes, stirring halfway through. 4. Once cooked, transfer the prawns and chorizo to a serving dish, drizzle with orange juice, and sprinkle with parsley. Enjoy your delicious Smoky Prawns and Chorizo Tapas!

Tandoori-Spiced Salmon and Potatoes

Prep time: 10 minutes | Cook time: 28 minutes | Serves 2

455 g Fingerling or new potatoes
2 tablespoons vegetable oil, divided
Kosher or coarse sea salt and freshly ground black pepper, to taste
1 teaspoon ground turmeric
1 teaspoon ground cumin
1 teaspoon ground ginger
½ teaspoon smoked paprika
¼ teaspoon cayenne pepper
2 (170 g) skin-on salmon fillets

1. Preheat the air fryer to 190ºC. 2. Toss the potatoes with 1 tablespoon of oil, salt, and pepper in a bowl. Transfer them to the air fryer and cook for 20 minutes. 3. In another bowl, combine the remaining 1 tablespoon of oil with turmeric, cumin, ginger, paprika, and cayenne. Coat the salmon fillets with the spice mixture. 4. After the potatoes have cooked for 20 minutes, place the salmon fillets, skin-side up, on top of the potatoes and continue cooking until the potatoes are tender and the salmon is cooked with slightly crisp skin. 5. Transfer the salmon fillets to plates and serve them with the warm potatoes. Enjoy your delicious Tandoori-Spiced Salmon and Potatoes!

Steamed Cod with Garlic and Swiss Chard

Prep time: 5 minutes | Cook time: 12 minutes | Serves 4

1 teaspoon salt
½ teaspoon dried oregano
½ teaspoon dried thyme
½ teaspoon garlic powder
4 cod fillets
½ white onion, thinly sliced
135 g Swiss chard, washed, stemmed, and torn into pieces
60 ml olive oil
1 lemon, quartered

1. Preheat the air fryer to 190ºC. 2. Whisk together salt, oregano, thyme, and garlic powder in a small bowl. 3. Tear off four pieces of aluminum foil. Place a cod fillet in the center of each foil sheet and sprinkle with the spice mixture. 4. Add onion slices and Swiss chard to each foil packet. Drizzle olive oil and lemon juice over the contents of each packet. 5. Fold and seal the sides of the foil packets, then place them in the air fryer basket. 6. Steam the packets for 12 minutes. 7. Remove the packets from the air fryer and carefully open them to avoid steam burns. Enjoy your delicious Steamed Cod with Garlic and Swiss Chard!

Baked Tilapia with Garlic Aioli

Prep time: 5 minutes | Cook time: 15 minutes | Serves 4

Tilapia:
4 tilapia fillets
1 tablespoon extra-virgin olive oil
1 teaspoon garlic powder
1 teaspoon paprika
1 teaspoon dried basil
A pinch of lemon-pepper
seasoning
Garlic Aioli:
2 garlic cloves, minced
1 tablespoon mayonnaise
Juice of ½ lemon
1 teaspoon extra-virgin olive oil
Salt and pepper, to taste

1. Preheat the air fryer to 200ºC. 2. Brush both sides of each tilapia fillet with olive oil and sprinkle with garlic powder, paprika, basil, and lemon-pepper seasoning. 3. Place the seasoned fillets in the air fryer basket and bake for 15 minutes, flipping them halfway through, until the fish flakes easily and is cooked through. 4. In the meantime, prepare the garlic aioli by whisking together garlic, mayo, lemon juice, olive oil, salt, and pepper in a small bowl until smooth. 5. Once the tilapia is done, remove it from the air fryer and serve with the garlic aioli on the side. Enjoy your delicious Baked Tilapia with Garlic Aioli!

Sea Bass with Avocado Cream

Prep time: 30 minutes | Cook time: 9 minutes | Serves 4

Fish Fillets:
1½ tablespoons balsamic vinegar
120 ml vegetable broth
⅓ teaspoon shallot powder
1 tablespoon coconut aminos, or tamari
4 Sea Bass fillets
1 teaspoon ground black pepper
1½ tablespoons olive oil
Fine sea salt, to taste
⅓ teaspoon garlic powder

Avocado Cream:
2 tablespoons Greek-style yogurt
1 clove garlic, peeled and minced
1 teaspoon ground black pepper
½ tablespoon olive oil
80 ml vegetable broth
1 avocado
½ teaspoon lime juice
⅓ teaspoon fine sea salt

1. In a bowl, season the sea bass fillets with the specified seasonings and mix well. In a separate bowl, combine the remaining ingredients to create a marinade for the fish. 2. Place the seasoned sea bass fillets in the marinade, ensuring they are well coated. Cover the bowl and refrigerate for at least 3 hours to allow the fillets to marinate. 3. Preheat the air fryer to 160°C. Arrange the marinated sea bass fillets in the air fryer grill basket and cook for 9 minutes. 4. While the sea bass is cooking, prepare the avocado sauce by blending all the sauce ingredients using an immersion blender or regular blender. 5. Once the sea bass is cooked, serve the fillets topped with the avocado sauce. Enjoy the delicious Sea Bass with Avocado Cream!

Fried Prawns

Prep time: 15 minutes | Cook time: 5 minutes | Serves 4

35 g self-raising flour
1 teaspoon paprika
1 teaspoon salt
½ teaspoon freshly ground black pepper
1 large egg, beaten

60 g finely crushed panko bread crumbs
20 frozen large prawns (about 900 g), peeled and deveined
Cooking spray

1. In a shallow bowl, whisk together the flour, paprika, salt, and pepper. In two separate shallow bowls, place the beaten egg and bread crumbs. 2. Dip each prawn into the flour mixture, then the egg, and finally the bread crumbs, ensuring they are thoroughly coated. 3. Preheat the air fryer to 200°C and line one of the air fryer baskets with baking paper. 4. Arrange the coated prawns on the baking paper and spritz them with oil. 5. Air fry for 2 minutes, shake the basket, spritz the prawns with more oil, and continue air frying for 3 more minutes until they are lightly browned and crispy. Serve the fried prawns hot and enjoy!

Baked Monkfish

Prep time: 20 minutes | Cook time: 12 minutes | Serves 2

2 teaspoons olive oil
100 g celery, sliced
2 bell peppers, sliced
1 teaspoon dried thyme
½ teaspoon dried marjoram
½ teaspoon dried rosemary
2 monkfish fillets
1 tablespoon coconut aminos,

or tamari
2 tablespoons lime juice
Coarse salt and ground black pepper, to taste
1 teaspoon cayenne pepper
90 g Kalamata olives, pitted and sliced

1. Heat olive oil in a nonstick skillet and sauté celery and peppers until tender. Sprinkle with thyme, marjoram, and rosemary, then set aside. 2. In a separate bowl, coat the fish fillets with coconut aminos, lime juice, salt, black pepper, and cayenne pepper. Place the fillets in the greased air fryer basket and bake at 200°C for 8 minutes. 3. Flip the fillets, add olives, and cook for an additional 4 minutes. Serve the baked monkfish with the sautéed vegetables on the side. Enjoy your meal!

Butter-Wine Baked Salmon

Prep time: 5 minutes | Cook time: 10 minutes | Serves 4

4 tablespoons butter, melted
2 cloves garlic, minced
Sea salt and ground black pepper, to taste
60 ml dry white wine or apple cider vinegar

1 tablespoon lime juice
1 teaspoon smoked paprika
½ teaspoon onion powder
4 salmon steaks
Cooking spray

1. Mix all the ingredients, except for the salmon and oil, in a shallow dish. Ensure they are well combined. 2. Add the salmon steaks to the dish, turning them to coat both sides with the marinade. Place the salmon in the refrigerator and let it marinate for 30 minutes. 3. Preheat the air fryer to 180°C. 4. Remove the salmon steaks from the marinade, discarding any excess. Place the salmon in one of the air fryer baskets and spray it with cooking oil. 5. Air fry the salmon for approximately 10 minutes, flipping the steaks halfway through the cooking time. Cook until the salmon reaches your desired level of doneness. 6. Once cooked, divide the salmon steaks onto four plates and serve. Enjoy your delicious Butter-Wine Baked Salmon!

Panko-Crusted Fish Sticks

Prep time: 10 minutes | Cook time: 15 minutes | Serves 4

Tartar Sauce:
470 ml mayonnaise
2 tablespoons dill pickle relish
1 tablespoon dried minced onions
Fish Sticks:
Olive or vegetable oil, for spraying
455 g tilapia fillets

40 g plain flour
60 g panko bread crumbs
2 tablespoons Creole seasoning
2 teaspoons garlic granules
1 teaspoon onion powder
½ teaspoon salt
¼ teaspoon freshly ground black pepper
1 large egg

1. In a small bowl, whisk together mayonnaise, pickle relish, and onions to make the tartar sauce. Cover and refrigerate until ready to serve. 2. Preheat the air fryer to 180ºC. Line one of the air fryer baskets with baking paper and lightly spray with oil. 3. Cut the fish fillets into equal-size sticks and place them in a zip-top plastic bag. 4. Add flour to the bag, seal, and shake well to coat the fish sticks. 5. In a shallow bowl, mix together bread crumbs, Creole seasoning, garlic, onion powder, salt, and black pepper. 6. Whisk the egg in a small bowl. 7. Dip the fish sticks in the egg, then coat them in the bread crumb mixture. 8. Place the coated fish sticks in the prepared basket, working in batches if needed. Spray lightly with oil. 9. Air fry for 12 to 15 minutes until the fish sticks are browned and cooked through. Serve the crispy fish sticks with the tartar sauce. Enjoy!

Maple Balsamic Glazed Salmon

Prep time: 5 minutes | Cook time: 10 minutes | Serves 4

4 fillets of salmon, 170 g each
Salt and freshly ground black pepper, to taste
Vegetable oil

60 ml pure maple syrup
3 tablespoons balsamic vinegar
1 teaspoon Dijon mustard

1. Preheat the air fryer to 200ºC. 2. Season the salmon with salt and black pepper, then place the fillets in one of the air fryer baskets that has been sprayed or brushed with vegetable oil. Air fry for 5 minutes. 3. In a small saucepan over medium heat, combine maple syrup, balsamic vinegar, and Dijon mustard. Stir well and let it simmer until slightly thickened. Be careful not to let it burn. 4. Brush the glaze onto the salmon fillets and air fry for an additional 5 minutes, until the salmon is firm to the touch and the glaze is nicely browned. Brush on more glaze before serving with rice, vegetables, or a green salad. Enjoy the delicious Maple Balsamic Glazed Salmon!

Coconut Prawns with Spicy Dipping Sauce

Prep time: 15 minutes | Cook time: 8 minutes | Serves 4

70 g pork scratchings
70 g desiccated, unsweetened coconut
45 g coconut flour
1 teaspoon onion powder
1 teaspoon garlic powder
2 eggs
680 g large prawns, peeled and deveined

½ teaspoon salt
¼ teaspoon freshly ground black pepper
Spicy Dipping Sauce:
115 g mayonnaise
2 tablespoons Sriracha
Zest and juice of ½ lime
1 clove garlic, minced

1. Preheat the air fryer to 200ºC. 2. In a food processor, pulse pork scratchings and desiccated coconut until coarse crumbs form. Transfer to a shallow bowl. 3. In another bowl, combine coconut flour, onion powder, and garlic powder. Mix well. 4. Whisk eggs in a third bowl until frothy. 5. Season prawns with salt and pepper in a large bowl, tossing gently to coat. 6. Dredge prawns in flour mixture, then dip in beaten eggs, and finally coat with pork rind crumb mixture. Arrange coated prawns on a baking sheet. 7. Working in batches if needed, place prawns in a single layer in the air fryer basket. Air fry for 8 minutes, turning halfway through, until cooked through. 8. For the spicy dipping sauce, whisk together mayonnaise, Sriracha, lime zest, lime juice, and garlic in a small bowl. Serve the sauce alongside the coconut prawns. Enjoy!

Asian Swordfish

Prep time: 10 minutes | Cook time: 6 to 11 minutes | Serves 4

4 swordfish steaks, 100 g each
½ teaspoon toasted sesame oil
1 jalapeño pepper, finely minced
2 garlic cloves, grated
1 tablespoon grated fresh ginger

½ teaspoon Chinese five-spice powder
⅛ teaspoon freshly ground black pepper
2 tablespoons freshly squeezed lemon juice

1. Drizzle sesame oil over the swordfish steaks on a work surface. 2. In a small bowl, mix jalapeño, garlic, ginger, five-spice powder, pepper, and lemon juice. Rub this mixture onto the fish and let it marinate for 10 minutes. 3. Roast the swordfish in the air fryer at 190ºC for 6 to 11 minutes, or until the internal temperature reaches at least 60ºC on a meat thermometer. Serve immediately and enjoy the flavorful Asian Swordfish.

Salmon with Provolone Cheese & Fish Taco Bowl

Prep time: 15 minutes | Cook time: 15 minutes

Salmon with Provolone Cheese | Serves 4

455 g salmon fillet, chopped	1 teaspoon avocado oil
60 g Provolone or Edam, grated	¼ teaspoon ground paprika

Fish Taco Bowl | Serves 4

½ teaspoon salt	cabbage
¼ teaspoon garlic powder	735 g mayonnaise
¼ teaspoon ground cumin	¼ teaspoon ground black
4 cod fillets, 110 g each	pepper
360 g finely shredded green	20 g chopped pickled jalapeños

Prepare for Salmon with Provolone Cheese:

1. Sprinkle the salmon fillets with avocado oil and put in zone 1.
2. Then sprinkle the fish with ground paprika and top with Provolone cheese.

Prepare for Fish Taco Bowl:

1. Sprinkle salt, garlic powder, and cumin over cod
2. place into ungreased zone 2.

Cook:

1. In zone 1, adjust the air fryer temperature to 180°C and air fry for 15 minutes.
2. In zone 2, adjust the air fryer temperature to 180°C and air fry for 12 minutes.
3. Press SYNC, then press Start.
4. For zone 2, cod will flake easily and have an internal temperature of at least 64°C when done. In a large bowl, toss cabbage with mayonnaise, pepper, and jalapeños until fully coated. Serve cod warm over cabbage slaw on four medium plates.

Lemony Prawns and Courgette

Prep time: 15 minutes | Cook time: 7 to 8 minutes | Serves 4

570 g extra-large raw prawns, peeled and deveined	1½ teaspoons dried oregano
2 medium courgettes (about 230 g each), halved lengthwise and cut into ½-inch-thick slices	⅛ teaspoon crushed red pepper flakes (optional)
	Juice of ½ lemon
1½ tablespoons olive oil	1 tablespoon chopped fresh mint
½ teaspoon garlic salt	1 tablespoon chopped fresh dill

1. Preheat the air fryer to 180°C. 2. In a large bowl, combine prawns, courgette, oil, garlic salt, oregano, and pepper flakes (if using). Toss to coat the ingredients evenly. 3. Working in batches, arrange a single layer of prawns and courgette in one of the air fryer baskets. Air fry for 7 to 8 minutes, shaking the basket halfway through cooking, until the courgette is golden and the prawns are cooked through. 4. Transfer the cooked prawns and courgette to a serving dish and tent with foil to keep warm. 5. Top with lemon juice, mint, and dill. Serve and enjoy the flavorful Lemony Prawns and Courgette.

Prawns

Prep time: 15 minutes | Cook time: 12 minutes

Honey-Glazed Salmon | Serves 4

60 ml raw honey	½ teaspoon salt
4 garlic cloves, minced	Olive oil cooking spray
1 tablespoon olive oil	4 (1½-inch-thick) salmon fillets

Lemony Prawns | Serves 4

455 g prawns, peeled and deveined	2 cloves garlic, finely minced
4 tablespoons olive oil	1 teaspoon crushed red pepper flakes, or more to taste
1½ tablespoons lemon juice	Garlic pepper, to taste
1½ tablespoons fresh parsley, roughly chopped	Sea salt flakes, to taste

Prepare for Honey-Glazed Salmon:

1. Preheat the air fryer to 190°C.
2. In a small bowl, mix together the honey, garlic, olive oil, and salt.
3. Spray the bottom of the air fryer basket with olive oil cooking spray, and place the salmon in a single layer on the bottom of zone 1.
4. Brush the top of each fillet with the honey-garlic mixture.

Prepare for Lemony Prawns:

1. Preheat the air fryer to 200°C.
2. Toss all the ingredients in a large bowl until the prawns are coated on all sides.
3. Arrange the prawns in zone 2.

Cook:

1. In zone 1, adjust the air fryer temperature to 160°C and air fry for 10 to 12 minutes, or until the internal temperature reaches 64°C.
2. In zone 2, adjust the air fryer temperature to 170°C and air fry for 7 to 8 minutes, or until the prawns are pink and cooked through.
3. Press SYNC, then press Start.

Scallops Gratiné with Parmesan

Prep time: 10 minutes | Cook time: 9 minutes | Serves 2

Scallops:
120 ml single cream
45 g grated Parmesan cheese
235 g thinly sliced spring onions
5 g chopped fresh parsley
3 cloves garlic, minced
½ teaspoon kosher or coarse sea salt
½ teaspoon black pepper
455 g sea scallops
Topping:
20 g panko bread crumbs
20 g grated Parmesan cheese
Vegetable oil spray
For Serving:
Lemon wedges
Crusty French bread (optional)

1. In a baking pan, combine single cream, cheese, spring onions, parsley, garlic, salt, and pepper. Stir in the scallops. 2. In a small bowl, combine bread crumbs and cheese for the topping. Sprinkle the mixture evenly over the scallops. Spray the topping with vegetable oil. 3. Place the pan in one of the air fryer baskets and set the temperature to 160ºC for 6 minutes. Then increase the temperature to 200ºC and cook for an additional 3 minutes until the topping is nicely browned. 4. To serve, squeeze lemon wedges over the gratin and accompany with crusty French bread, if desired. Enjoy the delicious Scallops Gratiné with Parmesan!

Oyster Po'Boy

Prep time: 20 minutes | Cook time: 5 minutes | Serves 4

55 g plain flour
20 g yellow cornmeal
1 tablespoon Cajun seasoning
1 teaspoon salt
2 large eggs, beaten
1 teaspoon hot sauce
455 g pre-shucked oysters
1 (12-inch) French baguette, quartered and sliced horizontally
Tartar Sauce, as needed
150 g shredded lettuce, divided
2 tomatoes, cut into slices
Cooking spray

1. In a shallow bowl, whisk together flour, cornmeal, Cajun seasoning, and salt. In a separate shallow bowl, whisk eggs and hot sauce. 2. Dip the oysters in the cornmeal mixture, then in the egg mixture, and again in the cornmeal to coat thoroughly. 3. Preheat the air fryer to 200ºC and line one of the air fryer baskets with baking paper. 4. Place the coated oysters on the baking paper and spritz with oil. 5. Air fry for 2 minutes, then shake the basket, spritz the oysters with oil, and air fry for an additional 3 minutes until they are lightly browned and crispy. 6. Spread Tartar Sauce on each sandwich half, then assemble the po'boys by layering fried oysters, shredded lettuce, and tomato slices. 7. Serve the Oyster Po'Boys immediately and enjoy!

Honey-Glazed Salmon & Lemony Crab Cakes with Mango Mayo

Prep time: 25 minutes | Cook time: 15 minutes | Serves 4

Crab Cakes:
235 g chopped red onion
8 g fresh coriander leaves
1 small serrano chilli or jalapeño, seeded and quartered
230 g lump crab meat
1 large egg
1 tablespoon mayonnaise
1 tablespoon whole-grain mustard
2 teaspoons minced fresh ginger
½ teaspoon ground cumin
½ teaspoon ground coriander
¼ teaspoon kosher or coarse sea salt
2 tablespoons fresh lemon juice
45 g panko bread crumbs
Vegetable oil spray
Mango Mayo:
80 g diced fresh mango
115 g mayonnaise
½ teaspoon grated lime zest
2 teaspoons fresh lime juice
Pinch of cayenne pepper

1. In a food processor, mince the onion, coriander leaves, and serrano pepper. 2. In a large bowl, combine the minced vegetables with the crab meat, egg, mayonnaise, mustard, ginger, cumin, ground coriander, salt, lemon juice, and 60 g of bread crumbs. Mix gently until well combined. 3. Shape the mixture into four patties and coat each patty with the remaining 30 g of bread crumbs. 4. Arrange the crab cakes in the air fryer basket, spray with vegetable oil, and cook at 190ºC for 15 minutes. Flip the crab cakes halfway through the cooking time and spray the other side with vegetable oil to ensure even browning. 5. While the crab cakes are cooking, prepare the mango mayo by blending mango, mayonnaise, lime zest, lime juice, and cayenne until smooth. 6. Serve the warm crab cakes with the mango mayo. Enjoy your delicious Crab Cakes with Mango Mayo!

Scallops and Spinach with Cream Sauce

Prep time: 5 minutes | Cook time: 10 minutes | Serves 2

Vegetable oil spray
280 g frozen spinach, thawed and drained
8 jumbo sea scallops
Kosher or coarse sea salt, and black pepper, to taste

180 ml heavy cream
1 tablespoon tomato paste
1 tablespoon chopped fresh basil
1 teaspoon minced garlic

1. Spray a baking pan with vegetable oil spray and spread thawed spinach evenly in the pan. 2. Spray both sides of the scallops with vegetable oil spray, season with salt and pepper, and arrange them on top of the spinach. 3. In a small bowl, whisk together cream, tomato paste, basil, garlic, salt, and pepper. Pour the sauce over the scallops and spinach. 4. Place the pan in the air fryer and set it to 180°C for 10 minutes. Use a meat thermometer to check that the scallops have reached an internal temperature of 56°C. Enjoy your Scallops and Spinach with Cream Sauce!

Chapter 7 Desserts

Chapter 7 Desserts

Chocolate Soufflés

Prep time: 5 minutes | Cook time: 14 minutes |
Serves 2

Butter and sugar for greasing the ramekins
85 g semi-sweet chocolate, chopped
55 g unsalted butter
2 eggs, yolks and white separated

3 tablespoons granulated sugar
½ teaspoon pure vanilla extract
2 tablespoons All-purpose flour
Icing sugar, for dusting the finished soufflés
Heavy cream, for serving

1. Butter and sugar two 6-ounce ramekins. Melt the chocolate and butter together, then beat the egg yolks vigorously in a separate bowl. Add sugar, vanilla extract, and the melted chocolate mixture to the egg yolks, mixing well. Stir in flour until there are no lumps. 2. Preheat the air fryer to 160°C. 3. In another bowl, whisk the egg whites to soft peak stage. Gently fold the whipped egg whites into the chocolate mixture in stages. 4. Transfer the batter to the buttered ramekins, leaving a little space at the top. Place the ramekins into the air fryer basket and air fry for 14 minutes until the soufflés rise and turn brown on top. 5. Dust with icing sugar and serve immediately, optionally with heavy cream. Enjoy!

Chocolate Peppermint Cheesecake

Prep time: 5 minutes | Cook time: 18 minutes |
Serves 6

Crust:
110 g butter, melted
30 g coconut flour
2 tablespoons granulated sweetener
Cooking spray
Topping:

110 g unsweetened cooking chocolate
180 g mascarpone cheese, at room temperature
1 teaspoon vanilla extract
2 drops peppermint extract

1. Preheat the air fryer to 180°C and lightly coat a baking pan with cooking spray. 2. In a mixing bowl, whisk together the butter, flour, and sweetener until well combined. Transfer the mixture to the prepared baking pan and place it in the air fryer. Bake for 18 minutes until a toothpick inserted in the center comes out clean. 3. Remove the crust from the air fryer and let it cool on a wire rack. Once cooled, place it in the freezer for 20 minutes to firm up. 4. In a small bowl, combine all the ingredients for the topping and stir until well incorporated. 5. Spread the topping over the crust and return it to the freezer for another 15 minutes. 6. Serve the Chocolate Peppermint Cheesecake chilled. Enjoy!

Pumpkin Cookie with Cream Cheese Frosting

Prep time: 10 minutes | Cook time: 7 minutes |
Serves 6

25 g blanched finely ground almond flour
25 g powdered sweetener, divided
2 tablespoons butter, softened
1 large egg
½ teaspoon unflavoured gelatin
½ teaspoon baking powder
½ teaspoon vanilla extract

½ teaspoon pumpkin pie spice
2 tablespoons pure pumpkin purée
½ teaspoon ground cinnamon, divided
40 g low-carb, sugar-free chocolate chips
85 g full-fat cream cheese, softened

1. In a large bowl, mix almond flour and 25g sweetener. Stir in butter, egg, and gelatin until well combined. 2. Add baking powder, vanilla, pumpkin pie spice, pumpkin puree, and ¼ teaspoon cinnamon to the mixture, then fold in chocolate chips. 3. Pour the batter into a round baking pan and place the pan into the air fryer basket. 4. Adjust the temperature to 150°C and bake for 7 minutes, or until the top is golden brown and a toothpick inserted in the center comes out clean. Allow the cookie to cool for at least 20 minutes. 5. Meanwhile, prepare the cream cheese frosting by mixing cream cheese, remaining ¼ teaspoon cinnamon, and remaining 25g sweetener in a large bowl. Use an electric mixer to beat the ingredients until fluffy. 6. Once the cookie has cooled, spread the cream cheese frosting on top. Optionally, garnish with additional cinnamon. Enjoy!

Pecan Clusters

Prep time: 10 minutes | Cook time: 8 minutes |

Serves 8

85 g whole shelled pecans

1 tablespoon salted butter, melted

2 teaspoons powdered

sweetener

½ teaspoon ground cinnamon

½ cup low-carb chocolate chips

1. In a medium bowl, toss pecans with butter and sprinkle them with sweetener and cinnamon. 2. Place the pecans into the ungreased air fryer basket and adjust the temperature to 180ºC. Air fry for 8 minutes, shaking the basket two times during cooking. The pecans will initially feel soft but will become crunchy as they cool. 3. Line a large baking sheet with baking paper. 4. Melt the chocolate in a microwave-safe bowl, heating it in 20-second increments and stirring until fully melted. Place 1 teaspoon of melted chocolate on the baking sheet to form a rounded mound, then press a pecan into the top. Repeat this process with the remaining chocolate and pecans. 5. Place the baking sheet in the refrigerator and let the clusters cool for at least 30 minutes. Once cooled, store the Pecan Clusters in a sealed container in the refrigerator for up to 5 days. Enjoy!

Honeyed, Roasted Apples with Walnuts & Coconut Mixed Berry Crisp

Prep time: 10 minutes | Cook time: 20 minutes

Honeyed, Roasted Apples with Walnuts | Serves 4

2 Granny Smith apples

20 g certified gluten-free rolled oats

2 tablespoons honey

½ teaspoon ground cinnamon

2 tablespoons chopped walnuts

Pinch salt

1 tablespoon olive oil

Coconut Mixed Berry Crisp | Serves 6

1 tablespoon butter, melted

340 g mixed berries

65 g granulated sweetener

1 teaspoon pure vanilla extract

½ teaspoon ground cinnamon

¼ teaspoon ground cloves

¼ teaspoon grated nutmeg

50 g coconut chips, for garnish

Prepare for Honeyed, Roasted Apples with Walnuts:

1. Preheat the air fryer to 190ºC.

2. Core the apples and slice them in half.

3. In a medium bowl, mix together the oats, honey, cinnamon, walnuts, salt, and olive oil.

4. Scoop a quarter of the oat mixture onto the top of each half apple.

5. Place the apples in zone 1.

Prepare for Coconut Mixed Berry Crisp:

1. Preheat the air fryer to 160ºC. Coat a baking pan with melted butter.

2. Put the remaining ingredients except the coconut chips in the prepared baking pan. Put the pan in zone 2.

Cook:

1. In zone 1, adjust the air fryer temperature to 190ºC and air fry for 12 to 15 minutes, or until the apples are fork tender.

2. In zone 2, adjust the air fryer temperature to 160ºC and air fry for 20 minutes.

3. Press SYNC, then press Start.

Almond-Roasted Pears

Prep time: 10 minutes | Cook time: 15 to 20 minutes

| Serves 4

Yogurt Topping:

140-170 g pot vanilla Greek yogurt

¼ teaspoon almond flavouring

2 whole pears

4 crushed Biscoff biscuits

1 tablespoon flaked almonds

1 tablespoon unsalted butter

1. Stir almond flavouring into yogurt and set it aside. 2. Halve the pears and remove the core. 3. Place the pear halves in the air fryer basket with the skin side down. 4. Combine crushed biscuits and almonds, then spoon a quarter of this mixture into the hollow of each pear half. 5. Place a piece of butter on top of the biscuit mixture in each pear. 6. Roast at 180ºC for 15 to 20 minutes until the pears are cooked through but still slightly firm. 7. Serve the pears warm, topped with a dollop of yogurt. Enjoy!

Almond Butter Cookie Balls

Prep time: 5 minutes | Cook time: 10 minutes |

Makes 10 balls

70 g almond butter

1 large egg

1 teaspoon vanilla extract

30 g low-carb protein powder

15 g powdered sweetener

25 g desiccated unsweetened coconut

40 g low-carb, sugar-free chocolate chips

½ teaspoon ground cinnamon

1. In a large bowl, mix almond butter, egg, vanilla, protein powder, and sweetener. 2. Fold in coconut, chocolate chips, and cinnamon. Roll the mixture into 1-inch balls and place them in a round baking pan. 3. Place the baking pan in one of the air fryer baskets and adjust the temperature to 160ºC. Bake for 10 minutes. 4. Allow the cookie balls to cool completely before storing them in an airtight container in the refrigerator for up to 4 days. Enjoy!

Simple Pineapple Sticks

Prep time: 5 minutes | Cook time: 10 minutes |
Serves 4

½ fresh pineapple, cut into sticks
25 g desiccated coconut

1. Preheat the air fryer to 200°C. 2. Coat the pineapple sticks with desiccated coconut and place each stick in one of the air fryer baskets. 3. Air fry the pineapple sticks for 10 minutes. 4. Serve the pineapple sticks immediately. Enjoy!

Pecan Butter Cookies

Prep time: 5 minutes | Cook time: 24 minutes |
Makes 12 cookies

125 g chopped pecans
110 g salted butter, melted
30 g coconut flour

150 g granulated sweetener, divided
1 teaspoon vanilla extract

1. In a food processor, blend pecans, butter, flour, 100 g sweetener, and vanilla until a dough forms. 2. Shape the dough into twelve individual cookie balls. 3. Cut three pieces of baking paper to fit the air fryer basket. Place four cookies on each baking paper and place one piece with cookies into the air fryer basket. Set the air fryer temperature to 160°C and cook for 8 minutes. Repeat with remaining batches. 4. Allow the cookies to cool for 5 minutes on a serving plate. While still warm, dust the cookies with the remaining sweetener. Let them cool completely before serving. Enjoy!

Pineapple Wontons

Prep time: 15 minutes | Cook time: 15 to 18 minutes
per batch | Serves 5

225 g cream cheese
170 g finely chopped fresh pineapple

20 wonton wrappers
Cooking oil spray

1. Soften the cream cheese by microwaving it in a small bowl for 20 seconds on high power. 2. In a medium bowl, mix together the softened cream cheese and pineapple until well combined. 3. Lay out the wonton wrappers on a clean work surface. 4. Spoon 1½ teaspoons of the cream cheese mixture onto each wrapper, being careful not to overfill. 5. Fold each wrapper diagonally to form a triangle, then bring the bottom corners together and seal the open

edges. 6. Preheat the air fryer to 200°C with the crisper plate in the basket. 7. Once preheated, spray the crisper plate with cooking oil and place the wontons in the basket. Spray the wontons with cooking oil as well. 8. Air fry the wontons for 10 minutes, then flip them, spray with more oil, and continue cooking for an additional 5 to 8 minutes until golden brown and crispy. 9. If making multiple batches, repeat steps 7 and 8 for the remaining wontons. 10. Allow the cooked wontons to cool for 5 minutes before serving. Enjoy!

Olive Oil Cake

Prep time: 10 minutes | Cook time: 30 minutes |
Serves 8

60 g blanched finely ground almond flour
5 large eggs, whisked
175 ml extra-virgin olive oil

75 g granulated sweetener
1 teaspoon vanilla extract
1 teaspoon baking powder

1. In a large bowl, simply mix all the ingredients together until well combined. Pour the batter into an ungreased round nonstick baking dish. 2. Place the baking dish into the air fryer basket. Adjust the temperature to 150°C and bake for 30 minutes. The cake will turn golden on top and have a firm center when it's done. 3. Once the baking time is complete, let the cake cool in the dish for 30 minutes before slicing and serving. Enjoy your delicious Olive Oil Cake!

New York Cheesecake

Prep time: 1 hour | Cook time: 37 minutes | Serves 8

65 g almond flour
45 g powdered sweetener
55 g unsalted butter, melted
565 g full-fat cream cheese
120 ml heavy cream

340 g granulated sweetener
3 eggs, at room temperature
1 tablespoon vanilla essence
1 teaspoon grated lemon zest

1. Coat a baking pan with flour. 2. In a mixing bowl, combine almond flour, powdered sweetener, and melted butter to form a breadcrumb-like mixture. Press it into the bottom of the pan to create a crust and bake until golden brown. Let it cool completely. 3. In a mixer, combine soft cheese, heavy cream, and granulated sweetener until creamy. Add eggs, vanilla, and lemon zest, mixing until fully combined. 4. Pour the filling over the cooled crust and spread evenly. 5. Bake in the preheated air fryer until set. 6. Allow the cheesecake to cool in the air fryer, then cover and refrigerate for at least 6 hours or overnight. Serve chilled. Enjoy your delicious New York Cheesecake!

Protein Powder Doughnut Holes

Prep time: 25 minutes | Cook time: 6 minutes | Makes 12 holes

25g blanched finely ground almond flour

30 g low-carb vanilla protein powder

100 g granulated sweetener

½ teaspoon baking powder

1 large egg

5 tablespoons unsalted butter, melted

½ teaspoon vanilla extract

1. Mix all the ingredients in a large bowl and place the mixture in the freezer for 20 minutes to firm up. 2. Wet your hands with water and roll the chilled dough into twelve balls. 3. Cut a piece of baking paper to fit your air fryer basket and place the doughnut holes on top of it. 4. Set the air fryer temperature to 190ºC and air fry the doughnut holes for 6 minutes. 5. Flip the doughnut holes halfway through the cooking time for even browning. 6. Allow the doughnut holes to cool completely before serving. Enjoy these tasty protein-packed treats!

Rhubarb and Strawberry Crumble

Prep time: 10 minutes | Cook time: 12 to 17 minutes | Serves 6

250 g sliced fresh strawberries

95 g sliced rhubarb

40 g granulated sugar

30 g quick-cooking oatmeal

25 g whole-wheat pastry flour, or All-purpose flour

40 g packed light brown sugar

½ teaspoon ground cinnamon

3 tablespoons unsalted butter, melted

1. Preheat the air fryer to 190ºC by inserting the crisper plate into the basket and placing it in the unit. 2. In a round metal baking pan, combine the strawberries, rhubarb, and granulated sugar. 3. In a separate medium bowl, mix together the oatmeal, flour, brown sugar, and cinnamon until well combined. Stir in the melted butter to create a crumbly mixture. Sprinkle this crumble mixture over the fruit in the baking pan. 4. Once the air fryer is preheated, place the baking pan into the basket. 5. Air fry for 12 minutes, then check the crumble. If the fruit is bubbling and the topping is golden brown, it is done. If not, continue cooking. 6. When the crumble is cooked to your desired level, remove it from the air fryer and serve it warm. Enjoy the delicious combination of rhubarb and strawberry flavors with a crunchy crumble topping!

Chapter 8 Snacks and Appetizers

Chapter 8 Snacks and Appetizers

Bruschetta with Basil Pesto

Prep time: 10 minutes | Cook time: 5 to 11 minutes |
Serves 4

8 slices French bread, ½ inch thick	cheese cheese
2 tablespoons softened butter	120 g basil pesto
120 g shredded mozzarella	240 g chopped cherry tomatoes
	2 spring onions, thinly sliced

1. Preheat the air fryer to 180ºC. 2. Spread butter on the bread slices and place them butter-side up in one of the air fryer baskets. Bake for 3 to 5 minutes, or until the bread becomes light golden. 3. Remove the bread from the basket and top each piece with cheese. Return the bread to the basket in two batches and bake for an additional 1 to 3 minutes, or until the cheese melts. 4. While the bread is in the air fryer, combine the pesto, tomatoes, and spring onions in a small bowl. 5. Once the cheese has melted, remove the bread from the air fryer and transfer it to a serving plate. Top each slice with the pesto mixture. Serve and enjoy your delicious bruschetta with basil pesto.

Spinach and Crab Meat Cups

Prep time: 10 minutes | Cook time: 10 minutes |
Makes 30 cups

1 (170 g) can crab meat, drained to yield 80 g meat	¼ teaspoon lemon juice
30 g frozen spinach, thawed, drained, and chopped	½ teaspoon Worcestershire sauce
1 clove garlic, minced	30 mini frozen filo shells, thawed
84 g grated Parmesan cheese	Cooking spray
3 tablespoons plain yoghurt	

1. Preheat the air fryer to 200ºC. 2. Ensure that the crab meat is free from any shell fragments. 3. In a mixing bowl, combine the crab meat, spinach, garlic, and cheese. 4. Add the yoghurt, lemon juice, and Worcestershire sauce to the mixture and thoroughly mix everything together. 5. Spoon a teaspoon of the filling into each filo shell. 6. Lightly spray one of the air fryer baskets with cooking spray and arrange half of the filled shells in the basket. Air fry for 5 minutes until the shells turn crispy and golden. Repeat this step

with the remaining shells. 7. Serve the spinach and crab meat cups immediately, and enjoy their delicious flavors.

Poutine with Waffle Fries & Kale Chips with Sesame

Prep time: 25 minutes | Cook time: 17 minutes |
Serves 4

Poutine with Waffle Fries | Serves 4

225 g frozen waffle cut fries	2 spring onions, sliced
2 teaspoons olive oil	90 g shredded Swiss cheese
1 red pepper, chopped	120 ml bottled chicken gravy

Kale Chips with Sesame | Serves 5

2L deribbed kale leaves, torn into 2-inch pieces	¼ teaspoon garlic powder
1½ tablespoons olive oil	½ teaspoon paprika
¾ teaspoon chili powder	2 teaspoons sesame seeds

Prepare for Poutine with Waffle Fries:

1. Preheat the air fryer to 190ºC.
2. Toss the waffle fries with the olive oil and place in zone 1.

Prepare for Kale Chips with Sesame:

1. Preheat air fryer to 180ºC.
2. In a large bowl, toss the kale with the olive oil, chili powder, garlic powder, paprika, and sesame seeds until well coated.
3. Put the kale in zone 2 and air fry for 8 minutes.

Cook:

1. In zone 1, adjust the air fryer temperature to 190ºC and air fry for 10 to 12 minutes.
2. In zone 2, adjust the air fryer temperature to 180ºC and air fry for 8 minutes.
3. Press SYNC, then press Start.
4. For zone 1, transfer the fries to a baking pan and top with the pepper, spring onions, and cheese. Air fry for 3 minutes, or until mixed vegetables are crisp and tender. Remove the pan from the air fryer and drizzle the gravy over the fries. Air fry for 2 minutes, or until the gravy is hot. Serve immediately.
5. For zone 2, flipping the kale twice during cooking, or until the kale is crispy. Serve warm.

Pickle Chips

Prep time: 30 minutes | Cook time: 12 minutes | Serves 4

Oil, for spraying
40 g sliced fresh dill or 240 g sweet gherkins, drained
240 ml buttermilk

245 g plain flour
2 large eggs, beaten
110 g panko breadcrumbs
¼ teaspoon salt

1. Line one of the air fryer baskets with baking paper and lightly spray it with oil. 2. In a shallow dish, combine the pickled cucumbers and buttermilk, allowing them to soak for at least 1 hour. Drain the cucumbers afterwards. 3. Set up three separate bowls with flour, beaten eggs, and breadcrumbs. 4. Coat each pickle chip lightly with flour, then dip it in the beaten eggs, and finally dredge it in the breadcrumbs, ensuring an even coating. 5. Place the coated pickle chips in the prepared basket, sprinkle them with salt, and lightly spray them with oil. Depending on the size of your air fryer, you may need to work in batches. 6. Air fry the pickle chips at 200ºC for 5 minutes, then flip them and continue cooking for an additional 5 to 7 minutes, or until they are crispy. Serve the pickle chips hot and enjoy their delicious crunchiness.

Italian Rice Balls

Prep time: 20 minutes | Cook time: 10 minutes | Makes 8 rice balls

355 g cooked sticky rice
½ teaspoon Italian seasoning blend
¾ teaspoon salt, divided
8 black olives, pitted
28 g mozzarella cheese cheese,

cut into tiny pieces (small enough to stuff into olives)
2 eggs
35 g Italian breadcrumbs
55 g panko breadcrumbs
Cooking spray

1. Preheat the air fryer to 200ºC. 2. Stuff each black olive with a piece of mozzarella cheese and set them aside. 3. In a bowl, combine the cooked sticky rice, Italian seasoning blend, and ½ teaspoon of salt. Stir well to mix all the ingredients together. Shape the rice mixture into a log and divide it into 8 equal portions. Mold each portion around a stuffed olive, rolling it into a ball shape. 4. Place the rice balls in the freezer for 10 to 15 minutes to firm up. 5. Prepare three shallow dishes: one with Italian breadcrumbs, one with whisked eggs, and one with a mixture of panko breadcrumbs and the remaining salt. 6. One by one, roll each rice ball in the Italian breadcrumbs, then dip it in the whisked eggs, and finally coat it with the panko breadcrumb mixture. Ensure that each ball is thoroughly coated. 7. Arrange the coated rice balls in one of the air fryer baskets and spritz both sides with cooking spray. 8. Air fry the rice balls at 200ºC for 10 minutes, or until they turn golden brown.

Flip the balls halfway through the cooking time to ensure even browning. 9. Once cooked, serve the Italian rice balls warm and enjoy their crispy exterior and gooey mozzarella filling.

Crunchy Tex-Mex Tortilla Chips

Prep time: 5 minutes | Cook time: 5 minutes | Serves 4

Olive oil
½ teaspoon salt
½ teaspoon cumin powder
½ teaspoon chili powder

½ teaspoon paprika
Pinch cayenne pepper
8 (6-inch) sweetcorn tortillas, each cut into 6 wedges

1. Spray the air fryer basket lightly with olive oil to prevent sticking. 2. In a small bowl, combine salt, cumin, chili powder, paprika, and cayenne pepper to create a flavorful seasoning mixture. 3. Place tortilla wedges in a single layer in one of the air fryer baskets. Lightly spray the tortillas with oil and sprinkle them with some of the seasoning mixture. You may need to cook the tortillas in multiple batches depending on the size of your air fryer. 4. Air fry the tortilla chips at 190ºC for 2 to 3 minutes. Shake the basket to ensure even cooking, and continue air frying until the chips are light brown and crispy, for an additional 2 to 3 minutes. Keep a close eye on the chips to prevent them from burning. Once they are ready, remove the chips from the air fryer and let them cool slightly before serving. Enjoy your crunchy Tex-Mex tortilla chips as a delicious snack or with your favorite dip.

Air Fried Pot Stickers

Prep time: 10 minutes | Cook time: 18 to 20 minutes | Makes 30 pot stickers

35 g finely chopped cabbage
30 g finely chopped red pepper
2 spring onions, finely chopped
1 egg, beaten
2 tablespoons cocktail sauce

2 teaspoons low-salt soy sauce
30 wonton wrappers
1 tablespoon water, for brushing the wrappers

1. Preheat the air fryer to 180ºC. 2. In a small bowl, combine the cabbage, pepper, spring onions, egg, cocktail sauce, and soy sauce, mixing well to combine all the ingredients. 3. Place approximately 1 teaspoon of the mixture in the center of each wonton wrapper. Fold the wrapper in half to cover the filling, and moisten the edges with water to seal them. You can crimp the edges with your fingers for an authentic pot sticker appearance. Lightly brush the pot stickers with water. 4. Arrange the pot stickers in one of the air fryer baskets, making sure they are not overcrowded. Air fry them in two batches for 9 to 10 minutes, or until they are heated through and the bottoms are lightly browned. 5. Serve the pot stickers hot and enjoy their delicious flavors.

Rumaki

283 g raw chicken livers
1 can sliced water chestnuts, drained

60 ml low-salt teriyaki sauce
12 slices turkey bacon

1. Begin by cutting the livers into 1½-inch pieces, making sure to trim out any tough veins as you slice. 2. In a small container with a lid, combine the livers, water chestnuts, and teriyaki sauce. If needed, add an additional tablespoon of teriyaki sauce to ensure that the livers are fully covered. Refrigerate the mixture for 1 hour to marinate. 3. Once marinated, cut the bacon slices in half crosswise. 4. Take one piece of liver and one slice of water chestnut and wrap them together with a half strip of bacon. Secure the bundle with a cocktail stick. Repeat this process until all the livers are wrapped. 5. Place the first batch of wrapped livers in one of the air fryer baskets, ensuring they are arranged in a single layer. 6. Air fry at 200ºC for 10 to 12 minutes, or until the liver is cooked through and the bacon is crispy. 7. While the first batch cooks, wrap the remaining livers. Once the first batch is done, remove them from the air fryer and repeat step 6 to cook the second batch. Enjoy these delicious Rumaki as an appetizer or party snack!

Grilled Ham and Cheese on Raisin Bread

2 slices raisin bread or fruit loaf
2 tablespoons butter, softened
2 teaspoons honey mustard
3 slices thinly sliced honey

roast ham (about 85 g)
4 slices Muenster cheese (about 85 g)
2 cocktail sticks

1. Begin by preheating the air fryer to 190ºC. 2. Take both slices of bread and spread softened butter on one side of each slice. Place the bread on the counter with the buttered side facing down. Spread honey mustard on the other side of each slice. Layer 2 slices of cheese, followed by the ham, and then the remaining 2 slices of cheese on one slice of bread. Top with the other slice of bread, making sure the buttered side is on the outside. 3. Transfer the assembled sandwich to one of the air fryer baskets and secure it with cocktail sticks to hold it together. 4. Air fry the sandwich for 5 minutes. Then, carefully flip the sandwich over, remove the cocktail sticks, and air fry for another 5 minutes to ensure both sides are evenly toasted and the cheese is melted. 5. Once done, remove the sandwich from the air fryer and cut it in half. Serve and enjoy the delicious combination of grilled ham and cheese on raisin bread!

Black Bean Corn Dip

½ (425 g) can black beans, drained and rinsed
½ (425 g) can sweetcorn, drained and rinsed
60 g chunky salsa
57 g low-fat soft white cheese

40 g shredded low-fat Cheddar cheese
½ teaspoon cumin powder
½ teaspoon paprika
Salt and freshly ground black pepper, to taste

1. Start by preheating the air fryer to 160ºC. 2. In a medium-sized bowl, combine the black beans, sweetcorn, salsa, soft white cheese, Cheddar cheese, cumin, and paprika. Season with salt and pepper, and mix well until everything is evenly combined. 3. Spoon the mixture into a baking dish. 4. Place the baking dish into one of the air fryer baskets and bake for approximately 10 minutes, or until the dip is heated through. 5. Serve the dip hot and enjoy!

Hush Puppies

144 g self-raising yellow cornmeal
60 g plain flour
1 teaspoon sugar
1 teaspoon salt
1 teaspoon freshly ground black pepper

1 large egg
80 g canned creamed sweetcorn
216 g minced onion
2 teaspoons minced jalapeño chillies pepper
2 tablespoons olive oil, divided

1. Thoroughly combine the cornmeal, flour, sugar, salt, and pepper in a large bowl. 2. In a small bowl, whisk together the egg and sweetcorn, then pour the mixture into the bowl of cornmeal and stir to combine. Add minced onion and jalapeño chillies, and cover the bowl with plastic wrap. Refrigerate the mixture for 30 minutes. 3. Preheat the air fryer to 190ºC and line the basket with baking paper, lightly brushing it with 1 tablespoon of olive oil. 4. Scoop out the cornmeal mixture and form it into 24 balls, approximately 1 inch in size. Place half of the balls in zone 1 and the remaining half in zone 2 of the air fryer. In zone 1, select the Air Fry button and adjust the temperature to 190ºC, setting the time to 5 minutes. In zone 2, select the Match Cook option and press Start. 5. After 5 minutes, shake the basket and brush the hush puppies with the remaining 1 tablespoon of olive oil. Continue cooking for an additional 5 minutes until they turn golden brown. 6. Remove the hush puppies from the basket and serve them on a plate. Enjoy!

Spiralized Potato Nest with Tomato Tomato Ketchup

Prep time: 10 minutes | Cook time: 15 minutes | Serves 2

1 large russet potatoes or Maris Piper potato (about 340 g)
2 tablespoons mixed vegetables oil
1 tablespoon hot smoked paprika
½ teaspoon garlic powder
Rock salt and freshly ground black pepper, to taste

120 ml canned chopped tomatoes
2 tablespoons apple cider vinegar
1 tablespoon dark brown sugar
1 tablespoon Worcestershire sauce
1 teaspoon mild hot sauce

1. If you have a spiralizer, spiralize the potato. If not, cut the potato into thin ⅛-inch-thick matchsticks. Rinse the potatoes under cold water until the water runs clear. Spread them out on kitchen paper and pat them dry. 2. In a large bowl, combine the potatoes, oil, paprika, and garlic powder. Season with salt and pepper, then toss to coat the potatoes evenly. Transfer the potatoes to the air fryer and cook at 200°C for 15 minutes, shaking the basket halfway through, until the potatoes are browned and crisp. 3. Meanwhile, blend the tomatoes, vinegar, brown sugar, Worcestershire sauce, and hot sauce in a small blender until smooth. Pour the mixture into a saucepan or frying pan and simmer over medium heat until it reduces by half, for about 3 to 5 minutes. Transfer the homemade tomato ketchup to a bowl and let it cool. 4. Once the spiralized potato nest is done, remove it from the air fryer and serve it hot with the tomato ketchup. Enjoy your delicious spiralized potato nest with tangy homemade tomato ketchup as a tasty side dish or snack.

Authentic Scotch Eggs

Prep time: 15 minutes | Cook time: 11 to 13 minutes | Serves 6

680 g bulk lean chicken or turkey sausage
3 raw eggs, divided
100 g dried breadcrumbs,

divided
65 g plain flour
6 hardboiled eggs, peeled
Cooking oil spray

1. In a large bowl, combine the chicken sausage, 1 raw egg, and 40 g of breadcrumbs. Mix well until all ingredients are thoroughly combined. Divide the mixture into 6 equal portions and shape each portion into a long oval shape. 2. In a shallow dish, beat the remaining 2 raw eggs. Place the flour in a separate small bowl and the remaining 80 g of breadcrumbs in another small bowl. Roll each hardboiled egg in the flour, then wrap one of the chicken sausage portions around each egg, ensuring the egg is completely covered. 3. Roll each encased egg in the flour, dip it into the beaten eggs, and then coat it with breadcrumbs. 4. Preheat the air fryer to 190°C. Spray the crisper plate with cooking oil and place the eggs in a single layer on the plate. Spray the eggs with oil. Air fry at 190°C for 13 minutes, turning the eggs and spraying them with more oil halfway through the cooking time. The Scotch eggs should be browned and the chicken sausage thoroughly cooked. 5. Once cooked, remove the Scotch eggs from the air fryer and serve them warm. Enjoy these authentic Scotch Eggs as a tasty snack or appetizer!

Lemony Endive in Curried Yoghurt & Veggie Salmon Nachos

Prep time: 15 minutes | Cook time: 12 minutes

Lemony Endive in Curried Yoghurt | Serves 6

6 heads endive
120 ml plain and fat-free yoghurt
3 tablespoons lemon juice

1 teaspoon garlic powder
½ teaspoon curry powder
Salt and ground black pepper, to taste

Veggie Salmon Nachos | Serves 6

57 g baked no-salt sweetcorn tortilla chips
1 (142 g) baked salmon fillet, flaked
100 g canned low-salt black beans, rinsed and drained
1 red pepper, chopped

50 g grated carrot
1 jalapeño chillies pepper, minced
30 g shredded low-salt low-fat Swiss cheese
1 tomato, chopped

Prepare for Lemony Endive in Curried Yoghurt:

1. Wash the endives and slice them in half lengthwise.
2. In a bowl, mix together the yoghurt, lemon juice, garlic powder, curry powder, salt and pepper.
3. Brush the endive halves with the marinade, coating them completely. Allow to sit for at least 30 minutes or up to 24 hours.
4. Preheat the air fryer to 160°C.
5. Put the endives in zone 1.

Prepare for Veggie Salmon Nachos:

1. Preheat the air fryer to 180°C.
2. In a baking pan, layer the tortilla chips. Top with the salmon, black beans, red pepper, carrot, jalapeño chillies, and Swiss cheese.
3. Put in zone 2.

Cook:

1. In zone 1, adjust the air fryer temperature to 160°C and air fry for 10 minutes.
2. In zone 2, adjust the air fryer temperature to 180°C and air fry for 9 to 12 minutes.
3. Press SYNC, then press Start.

Caramelized Onion Dip with White Cheese

Prep time: 5 minutes | Cook time: 30 minutes |
Serves 8 to 10

1 tablespoon butter
one medium-sized onion, halved and thinly sliced
¼ teaspoon rock salt, plus additional for seasoning
113 g soft white cheese
120 ml soured cream

¼ teaspoon onion powder
1 tablespoon finely chopped fresh chives
Black pepper, to taste
Thickly sliced potato crisps or mixed vegetables crisps

1. Begin by placing the butter in a baking pan and placing the pan in the air fryer basket. Set the air fryer to 90ºC for 1 minute or until the butter has melted. Add the onions and salt to the pan. 2. Set the air fryer to 90ºC for 15 minutes, or until the onions are softened. Then, increase the temperature to 190ºC and continue cooking for an additional 15 minutes until the onions are a deep golden color. Stir the onions two or three times during the cooking process. Allow the onions to cool completely. 3. In a medium-sized bowl, combine the cooked onions with the soft white cheese, soured cream, onion powder, and chives. Season with salt and pepper to taste. Cover the bowl and refrigerate for 2 hours to allow the flavors to meld together. 4. Serve the dip with potato crisps or mixed vegetable crisps. Enjoy!

Ranch Oyster Snack Crackers

Prep time: 3 minutes | Cook time: 12 minutes |
Serves 6

Oil, for spraying
60 ml olive oil
2 teaspoons dry ranch dressing mix
1 teaspoon chili powder
½ teaspoon dried fresh dill

weed
½ teaspoon garlic powder
½ teaspoon salt
1 (255 g) bag water biscuits or low-salt biscuits

1. Begin by preheating the air fryer to 160ºC. Line the air fryer basket with baking paper and lightly spray it with oil. 2. In a large bowl, combine the olive oil, ranch dressing mix, chili powder, fresh dill, garlic, and salt. Mix well to create a flavorful seasoning mixture. Add the crackers to the bowl and toss them until they are evenly coated with the seasoning. 3. Divide the cracker mixture between both zones of the air fryer basket. 4. Cook the crackers for 10 to 12 minutes, making sure to shake or stir them every 3 to 4 minutes. Continue cooking until the crackers are crisp and golden. Once done, remove them from the air fryer and allow them to cool before serving. Enjoy your Ranch Oyster Snack Crackers!

Stuffed Figs with Goat Cheese and Honey

Prep time: 5 minutes | Cook time: 10 minutes |
Serves 4

8 fresh figs
57 g goat cheese
¼ teaspoon cinnamon powder

1 tablespoon honey, plus more for serving
1 tablespoon olive oil

1. Preheat the air fryer to 180ºC and line an 8-by-8-inch baking dish with baking paper. 2. In a large bowl, mix together goat cheese and honey until well combined. 3. Carefully slice each fig in half lengthwise and spoon a small amount of the goat cheese mixture into the center of each fig half. 4. Place the stuffed figs into the prepared baking dish. 5. Put the baking dish into one of the air fryer baskets and air fry for about 5 minutes, or until the figs are softened and the goat cheese is slightly melted. 6. Remove the dish from the air fryer and let the stuffed figs cool for a few minutes before serving. Enjoy these delicious and elegant stuffed figs as a snack or appetizer.

Garlic Edamame

Prep time: 5 minutes | Cook time: 10 minutes |
Serves 4

Olive oil
1 (454 g) bag frozen edamame in pods
½ teaspoon salt
½ teaspoon garlic salt

¼ teaspoon freshly ground black pepper
½ teaspoon red pepper flakes (optional)

1. Start by spraying one of the air fryer baskets lightly with olive oil to prevent sticking. 2. In a medium-sized bowl, add the frozen edamame and lightly spray them with olive oil. Toss the edamame to ensure they are evenly coated with the oil. 3. In a small bowl, mix together the salt, garlic salt, black pepper, and red pepper flakes (if using). Sprinkle this mixture over the edamame and toss until the seasoning is evenly distributed. 4. Place half of the seasoned edamame in the prepared air fryer basket, making sure not to overfill it. 5. Set the air fryer to cook at 190ºC for 5 minutes. Once the initial cooking time is up, shake the basket to ensure even cooking and continue cooking for an additional 3 to 5 minutes, or until the edamame starts to brown and become crispy. 6. Repeat the process with the remaining batch of edamame. 7. Once the Garlic Edamame is cooked to your desired level of crispiness, remove them from the air fryer and serve immediately. Enjoy these flavorful and crunchy Garlic Edamame as a delicious and healthy snack!

Cheese-Stuffed Blooming Onion

Prep time: 10 minutes | Cook time: 15 minutes |
Serves 2

1 large brown onion (397 g)	3 tablespoons mayonnaise
1 tablespoon olive oil	1 tablespoon fresh lemon juice
Rock salt and freshly ground black pepper, to taste	1 tablespoon chopped fresh flat-leaf parsley parsley
18 g plus 2 tablespoons panko breadcrumbs	2 teaspoons wholemeal Dijon mustard
22 g grated Parmesan cheese	1 garlic clove, minced

1. Begin by placing the onion on a cutting board and trimming off the top. Peel off the outer skin, and then turn the onion upside down. Using a paring knife, cut vertical slits halfway through the onion at ½-inch intervals, making sure to keep the root intact. When you turn the onion right side up, it should open up like the petals of a flower. Drizzle the cut sides of the onion with olive oil and season with salt and pepper. Place the onion petal-side up in the air fryer and cook at 180ºC for 10 minutes. 2. While the onion is cooking, prepare the stuffing mixture. In a bowl, stir together the panko, Parmesan cheese, mayonnaise, lemon juice, parsley, mustard, and garlic until well combined, forming a smooth paste. 3. Once the onion has cooked for 10 minutes, remove it from the air fryer. Carefully stuff the paste all over and in between the onion petals. Make sure to evenly distribute the mixture. 4. Return the stuffed onion to the air fryer and cook at 190ºC until the onion is tender in the center and the bread crumb mixture is golden, approximately 5 minutes. 5. Remove the cheese-stuffed blooming onion from the air fryer, transfer it to a plate, and serve it hot. Enjoy this delicious appetizer!

Mexican Potato Skins

Prep time: 10 minutes | Cook time: 55 minutes |
Serves 6

Olive oil	beans
6 medium russet potatoes or Maris Piper potatoes, scrubbed	1 tablespoon taco seasoning
Salt and freshly ground black pepper, to taste	120 g salsa
260 g fat-free refried black	80 g low fat shredded Cheddar cheese

1. Begin by spraying the air fryer basket lightly with olive oil. 2. Take the potatoes and spray them lightly with oil, then season with salt and pepper. Use a fork to pierce each potato a few times.

3. Place the potatoes in the air fryer basket and air fry at 200ºC until they are fork-tender, which will take about 30 to 40 minutes depending on their size. Keep in mind that using a microwave or standard oven won't achieve the same crispy skin as the air fryer. 4. While the potatoes are cooking, mix the beans and taco seasoning in a small bowl, and set it aside until the potatoes are cool enough to handle. 5. Once the potatoes are ready, cut each one in half lengthwise. Scoop out most of the insides, leaving about ¼ inch in the skins to ensure they hold their shape. 6. Season the insides of the potato skins with salt and black pepper, and lightly spray them with oil. If necessary, cook the skins in batches. 7. Place the potato skins in the air fryer basket, half in zone 1 and the remaining in zone 2. In zone 1, select the Air Fry button and set the time to 8 to 10 minutes. In zone 2, select Match Cook and press Start. 8. Once the skins are done, transfer them to a work surface and spoon ½ tablespoon of seasoned refried black beans into each one. Top each with 2 teaspoons of salsa and 1 tablespoon of shredded Cheddar cheese. 9. Return the filled potato skins to the air fryer baskets in a single layer and lightly spray them with oil. 10. Air fry until the cheese is melted and bubbly, which will take about 2 to 3 minutes. Enjoy the delicious Mexican potato skins!

Lemony Pear Chips

Prep time: 15 minutes | Cook time: 9 to 13 minutes |
Serves 4

2 firm Bosc or Anjou pears, cut crosswise into ⅛-inch-thick slices	lemon juice
	½ teaspoon cinnamon powder
	⅛ teaspoon ground cardamom
1 tablespoon freshly squeezed	

1. Start by preheating the air fryer to 190ºC. 2. Separate the smaller stem-end pear rounds from the larger rounds that contain seeds. Remove the cores and seeds from the larger slices. Sprinkle all the pear slices with lemon juice, cinnamon, and cardamom, ensuring they are evenly coated. 3. Place the smaller pear chips into one of the air fryer baskets and air fry them for 3 to 5 minutes, or until they turn light golden, shaking the basket once during cooking to ensure even browning. Once done, remove the smaller chips from the air fryer. 4. Repeat the process with the larger pear slices, placing them in the air fryer basket and air frying them for 6 to 8 minutes, or until they also turn light golden, shaking the basket once during cooking. 5. Once both batches of pear chips are done, remove them from the air fryer and allow them to cool. You can then serve them immediately or store them in an airtight container at room temperature for up to 2 days. Enjoy these delightful and flavorful Lemony Pear Chips as a healthy snack!

Easy Spiced Nuts

Prep time: 5 minutes | Cook time: 25 minutes | Makes 3 L

1 egg white, lightly beaten
48 g sugar
1 teaspoon salt
½ teaspoon cinnamon powder
¼ teaspoon ground cloves

¼ teaspoon ground allspice
Pinch ground cayenne pepper
100 g pecan halves
135 g cashews
140 g almonds

1. In a bowl, combine the egg white, sugar, and spices. 2. Preheat the air fryer to 150°C. 3. Spray or brush one of the air fryer baskets with mixed vegetable oil. Toss the nuts in the spiced egg white mixture, ensuring they are well coated, and transfer them to the air fryer basket. 4. Air fry the nuts for 25 minutes, stirring them in the basket a few times during the cooking process. Check the nuts for crunchiness and toasting by tasting a few (be careful as they will be hot). If needed, air fry for a few more minutes. 5. Serve the spiced nuts warm or let them cool to room temperature. Store the nuts in an airtight container for up to two weeks. Enjoy your delicious and flavorful spiced nuts!

Old Bay Chicken Wings

Prep time: 10 minutes | Cook time: 12 to 15 minutes | Serves 4

2 tablespoons Old Bay or all-purpose seasoning
2 teaspoons baking powder
2 teaspoons salt

900 g chicken wings, patted dry
Cooking spray

1. Preheat the air fryer to 200°C and lightly spray one of the air fryer baskets with cooking spray. 2. In a large zip-top plastic bag, combine Old Bay seasoning, baking powder, and salt. Add chicken wings to the bag, seal it, and shake until the wings are fully coated in the seasoning mixture. 3. Lay the coated chicken wings in a single layer in the prepared air fryer basket and lightly mist them with cooking spray. If needed, cook the wings in batches to avoid overcrowding. 4. Air fry the wings for 12 to 15 minutes, flipping them halfway through the cooking time. Ensure that the wings are lightly browned and have reached an internal temperature of at least 74°C using a meat thermometer. 5. Transfer the cooked wings to a plate and repeat the process with the remaining chicken wings. 6. Serve the Old Bay chicken wings hot and enjoy their flavorful and crispy goodness.

Chapter 9 Vegetables and Sides

Chapter 9 Vegetables and Sides

Courgette Balls

Prep time: 5 minutes | Cook time: 10 minutes |
Serves 4

4 courgettes	1 tablespoon Italian herbs
1 egg	75 g grated coconut
45 g grated Parmesan cheese	

1. Start by grating the courgettes and make sure to remove all the moisture by drying them with a cheesecloth. 2. In a bowl, combine the grated courgettes with the egg, Parmesan cheese, Italian herbs, and grated coconut, mixing everything together until well incorporated. Shape the mixture into balls using your hands. 3. Preheat the air fryer to 200ºC. 4. Place the courgette balls in one of the air fryer baskets and air fry for approximately 10 minutes until they are golden and cooked through. 5. Once done, remove the courgette balls from the air fryer and serve them hot. Enjoy these delicious and healthy Courgette Balls as a flavorful snack or side dish.

Green Tomato Salad

Prep time: 10 minutes | Cook time: 8 to 10 minutes |
Serves 4

4 green tomatoes	2 teaspoons fresh lemon juice
½ teaspoon salt	2 tablespoons finely chopped
1 large egg, lightly beaten	fresh parsley
50 g peanut flour	1 teaspoon dried dill
1 tablespoon Creole seasoning	1 teaspoon dried chives
1 (140 g) bag rocket	½ teaspoon salt
Buttermilk Dressing:	½ teaspoon garlic powder
230 g mayonnaise	½ teaspoon onion powder
120 g sour cream	

1. Start by preheating the air fryer to 200ºC. 2. Slice the green tomatoes into ½-inch slices and sprinkle them with salt. Allow them to sit for 5 to 10 minutes. 3. In one small shallow bowl, beat the egg. In another small shallow bowl, combine peanut flour and Creole seasoning. Dip each tomato slice into the egg wash, then coat it with the peanut flour mixture, ensuring it is evenly coated. 4. Arrange the coated tomato slices in a single layer in one of the air fryer baskets. Lightly spray both sides of the slices with olive oil.

Air fry the tomatoes until they become browned and crisp, which usually takes around 8 to 10 minutes. You may need to work in batches if your air fryer is not large enough. 5. While the tomatoes are cooking, prepare the buttermilk dressing. In a small bowl, whisk together mayonnaise, sour cream, lemon juice, parsley, dill, chives, salt, garlic powder, and onion powder until well combined. 6. Once the tomato slices are ready, serve them on a bed of rocket or arugula, and serve the buttermilk dressing on the side. This refreshing Green Tomato Salad is a perfect combination of crispy tomatoes and creamy dressing, making it a delightful addition to any meal.

Easy Rosemary Green Beans & Roasted Aubergine

Prep time: 20 minutes | Cook time: 15 minutes |
Serves 1

Easy Rosemary Green Beans | Serves 1

1 tablespoon butter, melted	3 cloves garlic, minced
2 tablespoons rosemary	95 g chopped green beans
½ teaspoon salt	

Roasted Aubergine | Serves 4

1 large aubergine	¼ teaspoon salt
2 tablespoons olive oil	½ teaspoon garlic powder

Prepare for Easy Rosemary Green Beans:

1. Preheat the air fryer to 200ºC.

2. Combine the melted butter with the rosemary, salt, and minced garlic. Toss in the green beans, coating them well.

3. Put in zone 1.

Prepare for Roasted Aubergine:

1. Remove top and bottom from aubergine. Slice aubergine into ¼-inch-thick round slices.

2. Brush slices with olive oil. Sprinkle with salt and garlic powder. Place aubergine slices into zone 2.

Cook:

1. In zone 1, adjust the air fryer temperature to 200ºC and air fry for 5 minutes.

2. In zone 2, adjust the air fryer temperature to 200ºC and air fry for 15 minutes.

3. Press SYNC, then press Start.

Curry Roasted Cauliflower

Prep time: 10 minutes | Cook time: 20 minutes | Serves 4

65 ml olive oil
2 teaspoons curry powder
½ teaspoon salt
¼ teaspoon freshly ground black pepper

1 head cauliflower, cut into bite-size florets
½ red onion, sliced
2 tablespoons freshly chopped parsley, for garnish (optional)

1. Start by preheating the air fryer to 200°C. 2. In a large bowl, combine olive oil, curry powder, salt, and pepper. Add cauliflower florets and onion, gently tossing until the vegetables are evenly coated with the oil mixture. 3. Transfer the coated vegetables to the basket of the air fryer, spreading them out in a single layer. 4. Pause halfway through the cooking time to shake the basket, ensuring even cooking and browning. 5. Air fry the cauliflower and onion for a total of 20 minutes or until the cauliflower is tender and begins to brown. 6. Optional: Garnish with freshly chopped parsley for added freshness and flavor before serving. The curry-roasted cauliflower makes a delicious side dish or a flavorful addition to salads and grain bowls. Enjoy the aromatic blend of spices and the tender texture of the roasted cauliflower.

Butternut Squash Croquettes

Prep time: 5 minutes | Cook time: 17 minutes | Serves 4

⅓ butternut squash, peeled and grated
40 g plain flour
2 eggs, whisked
4 cloves garlic, minced
1½ tablespoons olive oil

1 teaspoon fine sea salt
⅓ teaspoon freshly ground black pepper, or more to taste
⅓ teaspoon dried sage
A pinch of ground allspice

1. Start by preheating the air fryer to 170°C. Line one of the air fryer baskets with parchment paper to prevent sticking. 2. In a mixing bowl, combine all the ingredients and stir until well combined, ensuring that the squash is evenly incorporated with the other ingredients. 3. Shape the mixture into small balls using a small cookie scoop or tablespoon, and place them onto a lightly floured surface. Use your hands to shape them into croquettes. 4. Transfer the croquettes to the lined air fryer basket, ensuring they are spaced apart to allow for even cooking. 5. Air fry the croquettes at 170°C for approximately 17 minutes, or until they turn golden brown and crispy. Cooking times may vary, so keep an eye on them to prevent overcooking. 6. Once cooked, carefully remove the squash croquettes from the air fryer basket and transfer them to a plate. Serve them warm as a tasty appetizer or side dish. Enjoy the crispy exterior and the flavorful butternut squash filling.

Roasted Radishes with Sea Salt

Prep time: 5 minutes | Cook time: 18 minutes | Serves 4

450 g radishes, ends trimmed if needed

2 tablespoons olive oil
½ teaspoon sea salt

1. Start by preheating the air fryer to 180°C. 2. In a large bowl, combine the radishes with olive oil and sea salt, ensuring that the radishes are evenly coated. 3. Pour the seasoned radishes into the air fryer basket and roast them for 10 minutes. 4. After 10 minutes, stir or turn the radishes over to ensure even cooking. Continue roasting for an additional 8 minutes, or until the radishes are tender and lightly browned. 5. Once roasted to your desired level of doneness, remove the radishes from the air fryer and serve them as a delicious side dish or a flavorful addition to salads or grain bowls. The roasted radishes with sea salt offer a unique twist to this root vegetable, bringing out their natural flavors and adding a touch of crispy texture. Enjoy the delightful taste of this simple and healthy dish.

Rosemary-Roasted Red Potatoes

Prep time: 5 minutes | Cook time: 20 minutes | Serves 6

450 g red potatoes, quartered
65 ml olive oil
½ teaspoon coarse sea salt

¼ teaspoon black pepper
1 garlic clove, minced
4 rosemary sprigs

1. Start by preheating the air fryer to 180°C. This will ensure that the potatoes cook evenly and develop a crispy exterior. 2. In a large bowl, combine the red potatoes, olive oil, salt, pepper, and minced garlic. Toss the potatoes well to ensure that they are evenly coated with the seasoning mixture. 3. Transfer the seasoned potatoes to one of the air fryer baskets, spreading them out in a single layer. This will allow for proper airflow and even cooking. 4. Place sprigs of fresh rosemary on top of the potatoes, allowing the aromatic herb to infuse its flavors during the cooking process. 5. Roast the potatoes in the air fryer for 10 minutes. After this initial cooking time, stir or toss the potatoes to ensure that all sides are evenly cooked and crispy. 6. Continue roasting the potatoes for an additional 10 minutes, or until they are golden brown and tender on the inside. 7. Once the potatoes are cooked to your desired level of crispiness, remove the rosemary sprigs and transfer the potatoes to a serving dish. You can season them with additional salt and pepper, if needed. 8. Serve the delicious Rosemary-Roasted Red Potatoes as a side dish alongside your favorite main course. Enjoy the fragrant aroma and the savory flavors of this classic dish.

Chermoula-Roasted Beetroots

Prep time: 15 minutes | Cook time: 25 minutes |

Serves 4

Chermoula:
30 g packed fresh coriander leaves
15 g packed fresh parsley leaves
6 cloves garlic, peeled
2 teaspoons smoked paprika
2 teaspoons ground cumin
1 teaspoon ground coriander
½ to 1 teaspoon cayenne pepper
Pinch crushed saffron (optional)

115 g extra-virgin olive oil
coarse sea salt, to taste
Beetroots:
3 medium beetroots, trimmed, peeled, and cut into 1-inch chunks
2 tablespoons chopped fresh coriander
2 tablespoons chopped fresh parsley

1. Prepare the chermoula sauce by combining fresh coriander, parsley, garlic, paprika, cumin, ground coriander, and cayenne in a food processor. Pulse until coarsely chopped. Add saffron if desired and process until combined. Slowly add olive oil in a steady stream while the processor is running. Season with salt. 2. In a large bowl, coat the beetroots with ½ cup of chermoula sauce or enough to cover them evenly. 3. Arrange the beetroots in the air fryer basket and preheat to 190ºC. Roast for 25 to 30 minutes until tender. 4. Transfer the beetroots to a serving platter, sprinkle with chopped coriander and parsley, and serve. Enjoy the flavorful and tender Chermoula-Roasted Beetroots as a side dish or part of a larger meal.

Parmesan Mushrooms

Prep time: 5 minutes | Cook time: 15 minutes |

Serves 4

Oil, for spraying
450 g shitake mushrooms, stems trimmed
2 tablespoons olive oil
2 teaspoons granulated garlic
1 teaspoon onion powder

½ teaspoon salt
¼ teaspoon freshly ground black pepper
30 g grated Parmesan cheese, divided

1. Line one of the air fryer baskets with parchment paper and lightly spray it with oil to prevent sticking. 2. In a large bowl, toss the mushrooms with olive oil, garlic, onion powder, salt, and black pepper until they are evenly coated. 3. Place the seasoned mushrooms in the prepared basket, ensuring they are in a single layer. 4. Set the air fryer to 190ºC and roast the mushrooms for 13 minutes, allowing them to cook until they become tender and golden. 5. Sprinkle half of the Parmesan cheese over the mushrooms and continue cooking for an additional 2 minutes, or

until the cheese has melted and starts to turn golden. 6. Carefully transfer the cooked mushrooms to a serving bowl and sprinkle the remaining Parmesan cheese over the top. Toss the mushrooms gently to ensure they are evenly coated with the cheese. 7. Serve the Parmesan mushrooms immediately as a tasty appetizer or side dish. Enjoy!

Mexican Corn in a Cup

Prep time: 5 minutes | Cook time: 10 minutes |

Serves 4

650 g frozen corn kernels (do not thaw)
Vegetable oil spray
2 tablespoons butter
60 g sour cream
60 g mayonnaise
20 g grated Parmesan cheese (or feta, cotija, or queso fresco)

2 tablespoons fresh lemon or lime juice
1 teaspoon chili powder
Chopped fresh green onion (optional)
Chopped fresh coriander (optional)

1. Place the corn in the bottom of one of the air fryer baskets and spray it with vegetable oil spray. Set the air fryer to 180ºC and cook the corn for 10 minutes, allowing it to become tender and slightly charred. 2. Transfer the cooked corn to a serving bowl. Add the butter to the bowl and stir until it melts and coats the corn. 3. Add the sour cream, mayonnaise, cheese, lemon juice, and chili powder to the bowl with the corn and butter. Stir well to combine all the ingredients, ensuring the corn is evenly coated with the creamy and flavorful mixture. 4. Serve the Mexican Corn in a Cup immediately, garnishing with green onion and coriander if desired. This delicious dish is perfect as a side dish or a snack with a Mexican twist. Enjoy!

Bacon-Wrapped Asparagus

Prep time: 10 minutes | Cook time: 10 minutes |

Serves 4

8 slices reduced-sodium bacon, cut in half
16 thick (about 450 g) asparagus spears, trimmed of woody ends

1. Preheat the air fryer to 180ºC. 2. Take a stalk of asparagus and wrap a half piece of bacon around the centre of the stalk, ensuring it is tightly wrapped. Repeat this step for the remaining asparagus stalks. 3. If needed, work in batches to avoid overcrowding the air fryer basket. Arrange the bacon-wrapped asparagus in a single layer, seam-side down, in the basket. 4. Air fry for 10 minutes, or until the bacon becomes crisp and the asparagus stalks are tender. 5. Carefully remove the bacon-wrapped asparagus from the air fryer and serve hot as a delicious appetizer or side dish. Enjoy!

Ricotta Potatoes

Prep time: 15 minutes | Cook time: 15 minutes | Serves 4

4 potatoes
2 tablespoons olive oil
110 g Ricotta cheese, at room temperature
2 tablespoons chopped spring onions
1 tablespoon roughly chopped

fresh parsley
1 tablespoon minced coriander
60 g Cheddar cheese, preferably freshly grated
1 teaspoon celery seeds
½ teaspoon salt
½ teaspoon garlic pepper

1. Start by preheating your air fryer to 180°C. 2. Using a knife, pierce the skin of the potatoes to allow steam to escape during cooking. 3. Place the potatoes in one of the air fryer baskets and air fry them for 13 minutes. If they are not fully cooked at this point, continue cooking for an additional 2 to 3 minutes. 4. While the potatoes are cooking, prepare the stuffing by combining all the other ingredients in a bowl. Mix well until everything is evenly combined. 5. Once the potatoes are cooked, carefully cut them halfway through to create an opening. 6. Spoon equal amounts of the stuffing mixture into each potato, filling them generously. 7. Serve the Ricotta Potatoes hot, and enjoy the creamy and flavorful combination of ricotta cheese and potatoes.

Southwestern Roasted Corn

Prep time: 10 minutes | Cook time: 10 minutes | Serves 4

Corn:
240 g thawed frozen corn kernels
50 g diced yellow onion
150 g mixed diced bell peppers
1 jalapeño, diced
1 tablespoon fresh lemon juice
1 teaspoon ground cumin

½ teaspoon ancho chili powder
½ teaspoon coarse sea salt
For Serving:
150 g queso fresco or feta cheese
10 g chopped fresh coriander
1 tablespoon fresh lemon juice

1. In a large bowl, stir together the corn, onion, bell peppers, jalapeño, lemon juice, cumin, chili powder, and salt until well incorporated. 2. Pour the spiced vegetables into one of the air fryer baskets. Set the air fryer to 190°C for 10 minutes, stirring halfway through the cooking time. 3. Transfer the corn mixture to a serving bowl. Add the cheese, coriander, and lemon juice and stir well to combine. 4. Serve immediately and enjoy the flavorful and delicious Southwestern Roasted Corn. The combination of sweet corn, spices, and cheese makes it a perfect side dish or topping for various dishes.

Buttery Mushrooms

Prep time: 10 minutes | Cook time: 10 minutes | Serves 4

230 g shitake mushrooms, halved
2 tablespoons salted butter, melted

¼ teaspoon salt
¼ teaspoon ground black pepper

1. In a medium bowl, toss the mushrooms with butter until they are well coated. This will help to enhance their flavor and give them a rich, buttery taste. 2. Sprinkle the mushrooms with salt and pepper, adjusting the amount to taste. The salt will bring out the natural flavors of the mushrooms, while the pepper adds a hint of spice. 3. Place the seasoned mushrooms into the ungreased air fryer basket. Make sure they are spread out in a single layer for even cooking. 4. Adjust the temperature of the air fryer to 200°C and set the timer for 10 minutes. This will provide enough time for the mushrooms to cook and become tender. 5. Shake the basket halfway through the cooking process to ensure that the mushrooms cook evenly on all sides. This will help to achieve a consistent texture and flavor. 6. Once the cooking time is complete, the mushrooms should be tender and fragrant. Remove them from the air fryer and serve them warm. They make a delicious side dish or a topping for steaks, pasta, or salads. Enjoy the rich and buttery flavor of these perfectly cooked mushrooms!

Marinara Pepperoni Mushroom Pizza

Prep time: 5 minutes | Cook time: 18 minutes | Serves 4

4 large portobello mushrooms, stems removed
4 teaspoons olive oil
225 g marinara sauce

225 g shredded Mozzarella cheese
10 slices sugar-free pepperoni

1. Preheat the air fryer to 190°C. 2. Brush each mushroom cap with one teaspoon of olive oil, ensuring they are well coated. 3. Place the mushroom caps on a baking sheet and bake in the air fryer, stem-side down, for 8 minutes. 4. Remove the caps from the air fryer and evenly divide the marinara sauce, Mozzarella cheese, and pepperoni among them. 5. Return the filled mushroom caps to the air fryer and cook for an additional 10 minutes, or until the cheese is melted and the tops are browned to your liking. 6. Serve the Marinara Pepperoni Mushroom Pizzas hot and enjoy the delicious combination of flavors.

Curried Fruit

Prep time: 10 minutes | Cook time: 20 minutes | Serves 6 to 8

210 g cubed fresh pineapple
200 g cubed fresh pear (firm, not overly ripe)
230 g frozen peaches, thawed

425 g can dark, sweet, pitted cherries with juice
2 tablespoons brown sugar
1 teaspoon curry powder

1. Start by combining all the ingredients in a large bowl. Gently stir the mixture to ensure that the sugar and curry are evenly distributed among the fruits. 2. Pour the fruit mixture into a baking pan and place it in a preheated oven at 180ºC. Bake for 10 minutes to allow the flavors to meld together. 3. After 10 minutes, remove the pan from the oven and give the fruits a stir. Return the pan to the oven and continue baking for an additional 10 minutes. 4. Once cooked, remove the Curried Fruit from the oven and serve it hot. Enjoy the unique combination of sweet and savory flavors in this delightful dish!

Spinach and Cheese Stuffed Tomatoes

Prep time: 20 minutes | Cook time: 15 minutes | Serves 2

4 ripe beefsteak tomatoes
¾ teaspoon black pepper
½ teaspoon coarse sea salt
1 (280 g) package frozen chopped spinach, thawed and squeezed dry

1 (150 g) package garlic-and-herb Boursin cheese
3 tablespoons sour cream
45 g finely grated Parmesan cheese

1. Cut the tops off the tomatoes and carefully remove and discard the pulp using a small spoon. Season the insides of the tomatoes with ½ teaspoon of black pepper and ¼ teaspoon of salt. Invert the tomatoes onto paper towels and allow them to drain while you prepare the filling. 2. In a medium bowl, combine the spinach, Boursin cheese, sour cream, half of the Parmesan cheese, and the remaining ¼ teaspoon of salt and ¼ teaspoon of pepper. Stir well until all the ingredients are thoroughly combined. Spoon the filling mixture into each tomato, dividing it equally among them. Sprinkle the remaining half of the Parmesan cheese on top of each tomato. 3. Place the stuffed tomatoes in one of the air fryer baskets. Set the air fryer to 180ºC and cook for 15 minutes, or until the filling is hot and the tomatoes are tender. The air frying process will help to melt the cheese and infuse the flavors into the tomatoes. 4. Once the cooking is complete, carefully remove the stuffed tomatoes from the air fryer and serve them warm. These Spinach and Cheese Stuffed Tomatoes make a delicious and nutritious appetizer or side dish. Enjoy the combination of tangy Boursin cheese, savory spinach, and juicy tomatoes in every bite!

Parmesan-Thyme Butternut Squash

Prep time: 15 minutes | Cook time: 20 minutes | Serves 4

350 g butternut squash, cubed into 1-inch pieces (approximately 1 medium)
2 tablespoons olive oil
¼ teaspoon salt

¼ teaspoon garlic powder
¼ teaspoon black pepper
1 tablespoon fresh thyme
20 g grated Parmesan

1. Preheat the air fryer to 180ºC. 2. In a large bowl, combine the cubed squash with the olive oil, salt, garlic powder, pepper, and thyme until the squash is well coated. 3. Pour this mixture into one of the air fryer baskets and roast for 10 minutes. Stir the squash and continue roasting for an additional 8 to 10 minutes, or until the squash is tender and lightly browned. 4. Remove the squash from the air fryer and sprinkle it with freshly grated Parmesan cheese while it's still hot. Toss gently to evenly distribute the cheese. 5. Serve the Parmesan-Thyme Butternut Squash as a delicious and flavorful side dish. The combination of the sweet squash, aromatic thyme, and savory Parmesan cheese creates a delightful and satisfying dish. Enjoy!

Fig, Chickpea, and Rocket Salad

Prep time: 15 minutes | Cook time: 20 minutes | Serves 4

8 fresh figs, halved
250 g cooked chickpeas
1 teaspoon crushed roasted cumin seeds
4 tablespoons balsamic vinegar

2 tablespoons extra-virgin olive oil, plus more for greasing
Salt and ground black pepper, to taste
40 g rocket, washed and dried

1. Preheat the air fryer to 190ºC. 2. Grease one of the air fryer baskets lightly with oil and line it with aluminum foil. Place the figs in the basket and air fry for 10 minutes until they are tender and slightly caramelized. 3. In a separate bowl, combine the chickpeas and cumin seeds. 4. Once the figs are done, remove them from the air fryer and add the chickpeas to the basket. Air fry for an additional 10 minutes until the chickpeas are crispy. Allow them to cool. 5. While the chickpeas are cooling, prepare the dressing by mixing the balsamic vinegar, olive oil, salt, and pepper in a separate bowl. 6. In a salad bowl, combine the rocket with the cooled figs and chickpeas. 7. Drizzle the dressing over the salad and toss to coat the ingredients. Serve the Fig, Chickpea, and Rocket Salad and enjoy the delightful combination of flavors and textures.

Crispy Courgette Sticks

Prep time: 5 minutes | Cook time: 14 minutes | Serves 4

2 small courgette, cut into
2-inch × ½-inch sticks
3 tablespoons chickpea flour
2 teaspoons arrowroot (or
cornflour)
½ teaspoon garlic granules

¼ teaspoon sea salt
⅛ teaspoon freshly ground
black pepper
1 tablespoon water
Cooking spray

1. Preheat the air fryer to 200°C to ensure it's hot and ready for cooking. 2. In a medium bowl, combine the courgette sticks with chickpea flour, arrowroot, garlic granules, salt, and pepper. Toss the ingredients together to ensure that the courgette sticks are evenly coated with the dry mixture. Add water to the bowl and stir well to create a batter-like consistency. The batter will help create a crispy coating on the courgette sticks. 3. Spritz one of the air fryer baskets with cooking spray to prevent sticking. Transfer the coated courgette sticks to the basket, spreading them out in a single layer. Mist the courgette sticks with additional cooking spray to promote browning. 4. Place the basket in the preheated air fryer and cook for approximately 14 minutes. Remember to shake the basket halfway through the cooking time to ensure even browning. The courgette sticks should become crispy and nicely browned when done. 5. Once cooked, carefully remove the crispy courgette sticks from the air fryer and serve them warm. They make a delicious and healthier alternative to traditional fried snacks. Enjoy them as a tasty appetizer or as a side dish with your favorite dipping sauce.

Lemony Broccoli

Prep time: 10 minutes | Cook time: 9 to 14 minutes per batch | Serves 4

1 large head broccoli, rinsed
and patted dry
2 teaspoons extra-virgin olive
oil

1 tablespoon freshly squeezed
lemon juice
Olive oil spray

1. Cut off the broccoli florets and separate them, including the stems if desired. 2. Preheat the air fryer to 200°C and toss the broccoli with olive oil and lemon juice in a large bowl. 3. Spray the air fryer's crisper plate with oil, then place half of the broccoli in the basket. 4. Select the AIR ROAST function at 200°C for 14 minutes, shaking the basket after 5 minutes and checking for crisp-tender, slightly browned broccoli. 5. Transfer the cooked broccoli to a serving bowl, and repeat with the remaining batch. Serve immediately for a refreshing and flavorful side dish.

Rosemary New Potatoes

Prep time: 10 minutes | Cook time: 5 to 6 minutes | Serves 4

3 large red potatoes
¼ teaspoon ground rosemary
¼ teaspoon ground thyme
⅛ teaspoon salt

⅛ teaspoon ground black
pepper
2 teaspoons extra-light olive oil

1. Preheat the air fryer to 170°C. 2. Place the potatoes in a large bowl and sprinkle them with rosemary, thyme, salt, and pepper. Use a spoon to stir and distribute the seasonings evenly. 3. Add the oil to the potatoes and stir once more to coat them well. 4. Transfer the seasoned potatoes to the air fryer basket. 5. Air fry at 170°C for 4 minutes, then stir and break apart any potatoes that have stuck together. 6. Continue cooking for an additional 1 to 2 minutes or until the potatoes are fork-tender. Enjoy the aromatic and flavorful Rosemary New Potatoes as a delicious side dish to complement your meal.

Sesame Taj Tofu

Prep time: 5 minutes | Cook time: 25 minutes | Serves 4

1 block firm tofu, pressed and
cut into 1-inch thick cubes
2 tablespoons soy sauce
2 teaspoons toasted sesame

seeds
1 teaspoon rice vinegar
1 tablespoon cornflour

1. Preheat the air fryer to 200°C to ensure it is hot and ready for cooking. This will help achieve a crispy texture for the tofu. 2. In a bowl, combine the tofu cubes with soy sauce, sesame seeds, and rice vinegar. Mix well to ensure the tofu is evenly coated with the flavors. 3. Cover the tofu with cornflour, which will create a crispy outer coating when air fried. This step helps to enhance the texture and taste of the tofu. 4. Place the tofu in one of the air fryer baskets, ensuring they are arranged in a single layer for even cooking. 5. Air fry the tofu for 25 minutes, shaking the basket at five-minute intervals. This will help the tofu cook evenly on all sides and achieve a golden, crispy exterior. 6. Once the tofu is cooked to your desired level of crispiness, remove it from the air fryer. Serve the Sesame Taj Tofu immediately as a delicious and flavorful appetizer or as part of a main course. The combination of soy sauce, sesame seeds, and rice vinegar creates a delightful flavor profile that pairs well with various dishes. Enjoy the crispy and flavorful tofu bites!

Blistered Shishito Peppers with Lime Juice

Prep time: 5 minutes | Cook time: 9 minutes | Serves 3

230 g shishito peppers, rinsed
Cooking spray
Sauce:

1 tablespoon tamari or shoyu
2 teaspoons fresh lime juice
2 large garlic cloves, minced

1. Preheat the air fryer to 200°C to ensure it's hot and ready for cooking. Spritz one of the air fryer baskets with cooking spray to prevent sticking. 2. Place the shishito peppers in the prepared basket and spritz them with cooking spray. This will help them cook evenly and develop a nice blistered texture. 3. Roast the peppers in the air fryer for 3 minutes to start the cooking process. While the peppers are roasting, whisk together all the ingredients for the sauce in a large bowl. This will be used to add flavor and tanginess to the peppers. Set the sauce aside for now. 4. After the initial 3 minutes of roasting, shake the basket to ensure even cooking, and spritz the peppers with cooking spray once again. This will help them continue to brown and blister. 5. Roast the peppers for an additional 3 minutes, and then shake the basket once more. Spritz the peppers with cooking spray for the final time and continue roasting for another 3 minutes. This will ensure that the peppers are nicely blistered and browned. 6. Once the peppers are done, carefully remove them from the air fryer basket and transfer them to the bowl of sauce. Toss the peppers in the sauce until they are well coated. 7. Serve the blistered shishito peppers with lime juice immediately, while they are still warm and flavorful. They make a delicious and slightly spicy appetizer or side dish. Enjoy the zesty combination of blistered peppers and tangy lime juice!

Chapter 10 Vegetarian Mains

Chapter 10 Vegetarian Mains

Super Vegetable Burger

Prep time: 15 minutes | Cook time: 12 minutes |
Serves 8

230 g cauliflower, steamed and diced, rinsed and drained
2 teaspoons coconut oil, melted
2 teaspoons minced garlic
60 g desiccated coconut
120 g oats
3 tablespoons flour
1 tablespoon flaxseeds plus 3

tablespoons water, divided
1 teaspoon mustard powder
2 teaspoons thyme
2 teaspoons parsley
2 teaspoons chives
Salt and ground black pepper, to taste
235 g breadcrumbs

1. Preheat the air fryer to 200ºC. 2. In a large bowl, combine the cauliflower with all the ingredients, except for the breadcrumbs. Mix everything well until fully incorporated. 3. Shape the mixture into 8 equal-sized burger patties using your hands. 4. Coat each patty in breadcrumbs, ensuring they are evenly coated. 5. Place half of the patties in zone 1 and the remaining patties in zone 2 of the air fryer basket, arranging them in a single layer. 6. Air fry the burger patties for approximately 12 minutes, or until they become crispy and golden. 7. Once cooked, serve the Super Vegetable Burgers hot and enjoy!

Courgette-Ricotta Tart

Prep time: 15 minutes | Cook time: 60 minutes |
Serves 6

120 g grated Parmesan cheese, divided
350 g almond flour
1 tablespoon coconut flour
½ teaspoon garlic powder
¾ teaspoon salt, divided
60 g unsalted butter, melted

1 courgette, thinly sliced (about 475 ml)
235 g Ricotta cheese
3 eggs
2 tablespoons double cream
2 cloves garlic, minced
½ teaspoon dried tarragon

1. Preheat the air fryer to 170ºC to ensure it is ready for baking the tart. 2. Coat a round pan with olive oil to prevent sticking and set it aside. 3. In a large bowl, whisk together 60 g of Parmesan cheese, almond flour, coconut flour, garlic powder, and ¼ teaspoon of salt. Mix until well combined. 4. Stir in the melted butter until the mixture resembles coarse crumbs. 5. Press the dough firmly into the bottom and up the sides of the prepared pan, creating a crust for the tart. 6. Air fry the crust for 12 to 15 minutes, or until it begins to brown and become crisp. 7. Allow the crust to cool to room temperature. 8. While the crust is cooling, place the courgette slices in a colander and sprinkle them with the remaining ½ teaspoon of salt. Toss gently to distribute the salt and let them sit for 30 minutes. 9. Use paper towels to pat the courgette slices dry and remove excess moisture. 10. In a large bowl, whisk together the ricotta, eggs, double cream, garlic, and tarragon until well combined. 11. Gently stir in the courgette slices, ensuring they are evenly coated with the ricotta mixture. 12. Pour the cheese and courgette mixture into the cooled crust. 13. Sprinkle the remaining 60 g of Parmesan cheese over the top of the tart. 14. Increase the air fryer temperature to 180ºC. 15. Place the pan with the tart in the air fryer basket and air fry for 45 to 50 minutes, or until the tart is set and a tester inserted into the center comes out clean. 16. Once cooked, remove the tart from the air fryer and let it cool slightly. Serve the Courgette-Ricotta Tart warm or at room temperature, and enjoy the delightful combination of flavors and textures.

Sweet Pepper Nachos

Prep time: 10 minutes | Cook time: 5 minutes |
Serves 2

6 mini sweet peppers, seeded and sliced in half
180 g shredded Colby jack or Monterey Jack cheese

60 g sliced pickled jalapeños
½ medium avocado, peeled, pitted, and diced
2 tablespoons sour cream

1. Place the peppers into an ungreased round non-stick baking dish, ensuring they are evenly distributed. 2. Sprinkle the peppers with cheese, covering them evenly. Top with sliced jalapeños for an added kick of heat. 3. Place the baking dish into the air fryer basket, making sure it fits comfortably. 4. Adjust the temperature of the air fryer to 180ºC and set the timer for 5 minutes. Allow the nachos to bake until the cheese is melted and bubbly. 5. Once the cheese is melted and the nachos are cooked to your liking, carefully remove the baking dish from the air fryer. 6. Top the nachos with sliced avocado for a creamy and fresh addition. 7. Drizzle sour cream over the nachos, adding a tangy and cool element. 8. Serve the Sweet Pepper Nachos while they are still warm, allowing everyone to enjoy the gooey cheese, spicy jalapeños, creamy avocado, and tangy sour cream.

Cayenne Tahini Kale

Prep time: 5 minutes | Cook time: 15 minutes |
Serves 2 to 4

Dressing:	Kale:
60 ml tahini	1 Kg packed torn kale leaves
60 g fresh lemon juice	(stems and ribs removed and
2 tablespoons olive oil	leaves torn into palm-size
1 teaspoon sesame seeds	pieces)
½ teaspoon garlic powder	Rock salt and freshly ground
¼ teaspoon cayenne pepper	black pepper, to taste

1. Preheat the air fryer to 180ºC, ensuring it reaches the desired temperature before proceeding. 2. In a large bowl, prepare the dressing by whisking together the tahini, lemon juice, olive oil, sesame seeds, garlic powder, and cayenne pepper until well combined. 3. Add the kale leaves to the bowl and thoroughly massage the dressing into the leaves, ensuring they are coated evenly. 4. Season the kale with salt and pepper to enhance the flavors. 5. Arrange the kale in a single layer in one of the air fryer baskets, allowing sufficient space for air circulation. 6. Air fry the kale for approximately 15 minutes, or until the leaves are slightly wilted and crispy, monitoring closely to prevent burning. 7. Once the desired texture is achieved, carefully remove the kale from the air fryer basket. 8. Transfer the Cayenne Tahini Kale to a serving plate and serve immediately, allowing everyone to enjoy the crispy and flavorful kale.

Aubergine Parmesan

Prep time: 15 minutes | Cook time: 17 minutes |
Serves 4

1 medium aubergine, ends trimmed, sliced into ½-inch rounds	30 g cheese crisps, finely crushed
¼ teaspoon salt	120 ml low-carb marinara sauce
2 tablespoons coconut oil	120 g shredded Mozzarella
120 g grated Parmesan cheese	cheese

1. Sprinkle both sides of the aubergine rounds with salt and let them sit wrapped in a kitchen towel for 30 minutes. This helps remove excess moisture. 2. After 30 minutes, press the aubergine rounds to remove any remaining water. Then, drizzle coconut oil over both sides of the rounds. 3. In a medium bowl, combine the Parmesan cheese and cheese crisps. Mix well. 4. Press each aubergine slice into the mixture, ensuring both sides are coated. 5. Place the coated rounds into the ungreased air fryer basket. 6. Adjust the air fryer temperature to 180ºC and air fry the aubergine rounds for 15 minutes, flipping them halfway through the cooking time. 7. The rounds will become crispy around the edges when done. 8. Spoon marinara sauce over the rounds and sprinkle with Mozzarella cheese. 9. Continue cooking for an additional 2 minutes at 180ºC, or until the cheese has melted. 10. Serve the Aubergine Parmesan warm, and enjoy!

Mushroom and Pepper Pizza Squares

Prep time: 10 minutes | Cook time: 10 minutes |
Serves 10

1 pizza dough, cut into squares	¼ red pepper, chopped
235 g chopped oyster mushrooms	2 tablespoons parsley
1 shallot, chopped	Salt and ground black pepper, to taste

1. Preheat the air fryer to 200ºC. 2. In a bowl, combine the oyster mushrooms, shallot, pepper, and parsley. Mix well to evenly distribute the ingredients. 3. Season the mixture with salt and pepper according to your taste preferences. 4. Spread the mushroom and pepper mixture on top of the pizza squares, ensuring an even distribution of toppings. 5. Place the prepared pizza squares in the air fryer and bake for approximately 10 minutes, or until the crust is crispy and the toppings are cooked. 6. Once cooked, remove the pizza squares from the air fryer and serve them warm. Enjoy your Mushroom and Pepper Pizza Squares!

Pesto Spinach Flatbread

Prep time: 10 minutes | Cook time: 8 minutes |
Serves 4

235 g blanched finely ground almond flour	cheese
60 g soft white cheese	235 g chopped fresh spinach leaves
475 g shredded Mozzarella	2 tablespoons basil pesto

1. In a large microwave-safe bowl, combine the flour, soft white cheese, and Mozzarella. Microwave the mixture on high for 45 seconds, then stir to combine. 2. Fold in the spinach and microwave for an additional 15 seconds to wilt the spinach. 3. Stir the mixture until a soft dough ball forms. 4. Cut two pieces of parchment paper to fit the air fryer basket. 5. Divide the dough into two sections and press each section out on the ungreased parchment paper to create 6-inch rounds. 6. Spread 1 tablespoon of pesto sauce over each flatbread round and place the rounds on the parchment paper in the ungreased air fryer basket. 7. Adjust the air fryer temperature to 180ºC and air fry the flatbreads for 8 minutes, turning them halfway through the cooking time to ensure even browning. 8. The flatbreads will be golden and crisp when done. 9. Allow the flatbreads to cool for 5 minutes before slicing and serving. Enjoy your delicious Pesto Spinach Flatbread!

Quiche-Stuffed Peppers

Prep time: 5 minutes | Cook time: 15 minutes | Serves 2

2 medium green peppers
3 large eggs
60 g full-fat ricotta cheese

60 g diced brown onion
120 g chopped broccoli
120 g shredded medium Cheddar cheese

1. Cut the tops off the peppers and remove the seeds and white membranes using a small knife. 2. In a medium bowl, whisk together the eggs and ricotta cheese until well combined. 3. Add the chopped onion and broccoli to the egg mixture and stir to incorporate. 4. Pour the egg and vegetable mixture evenly into each pepper, filling them to the top. 5. Sprinkle grated Cheddar cheese on top of each stuffed pepper. 6. Place the stuffed peppers into a 1 L round baking dish and place the dish into one of the air fryer baskets. 7. Adjust the air fryer temperature to 180°C and bake the stuffed peppers for 15 minutes, or until the eggs are mostly firm and the peppers are tender. 8. Once fully cooked, remove the stuffed peppers from the air fryer. 9. Serve the quiche-stuffed peppers immediately. Enjoy this delicious and flavorful dish!

Crispy Aubergine Rounds

Prep time: 15 minutes | Cook time: 10 minutes | Serves 4

1 large aubergine, ends trimmed, cut into ½-inch slices
½ teaspoon salt
60 g Parmesan 100% cheese crisps, finely ground

½ teaspoon paprika
¼ teaspoon garlic powder
1 large egg

1. Sprinkle the aubergine rounds with salt and let them sit for a few minutes. 2. Place the rounds on a kitchen towel and allow them to rest for 30 minutes to draw out excess water. 3. Pat the aubergine rounds dry using the kitchen towel. 4. In a medium bowl, combine cheese crisps, paprika, and garlic powder, and mix well. 5. In a separate medium bowl, whisk the egg. 6. Dip each aubergine round into the egg mixture, ensuring it is well coated. Then, gently press the round into the cheese crisp mixture to coat both sides. 7. Place the coated aubergine rounds into the ungreased air fryer basket. 8. Adjust the air fryer temperature to 200°C and air fry the rounds for 10 minutes, turning them halfway through cooking to ensure even browning. 9. The aubergine rounds should be golden and crispy when done. 10. Serve the crispy aubergine rounds while still warm. Enjoy their delicious crunch and flavor!

Crispy Fried Okra with Chilli

Prep time: 5 minutes | Cook time: 10 minutes | Serves 4

3 tablespoons sour cream
2 tablespoons flour
2 tablespoons semolina
½ teaspoon red chilli powder

Salt and black pepper, to taste
450 g okra, halved
Cooking spray

1. Preheat the air fryer to 200°C. 2. Spray one of the air fryer baskets with cooking spray to prevent sticking. 3. In a shallow bowl, place the sour cream. This will act as a binding agent for the flour mixture. 4. In another shallow bowl, thoroughly combine the flour, semolina, red chilli powder, salt, and pepper. This will create a flavorful coating for the okra. 5. Take each piece of okra and dip it in the sour cream, ensuring it is well coated. This will help the flour mixture adhere to the okra. 6. Roll the okra in the flour mixture, making sure each piece is evenly coated. 7. Arrange the coated okra in the prepared air fryer basket, ensuring they are in a single layer. This will allow them to cook evenly and become crispy. 8. Air fry the okra for 10 minutes, flipping them halfway through the cooking time. This will ensure that both sides are golden brown and crispy. 9. Once the okra is golden brown and crispy, remove them from the air fryer and let them cool for 5 minutes before serving. This will allow them to set and become even crispier. 10. Serve the Crispy Fried Okra with Chilli as a delicious appetizer or side dish. Enjoy the crunchy texture and spicy flavor of this tasty treat!

Printed in Great Britain
by Amazon

32830575R00044